ARTIFACTS

of

MOROLAND MUSEUM

third edition
field guide

Author/Photographer
Bruce Jenkins

Graphic Artist
Jess Holloway

ARTIFACTS OF MOROLAND MUSEUM by Bruce Jenkins

Books may be purchased in quantity and/or special sales by contacting Moroland Museum at:

www.morolandmuseum.com
morolandmuseum@gmail.com

Published by: Moroland Museum
Author & Photography by: Bruce Jenkins
Graphic Artist by: Jess Holloway

First Edition

Printed in USA

This book is dedicated to

the people of the Philippines, their weapons and artifacts,

our families and the to all our friends of Moroland.

God bless you all!

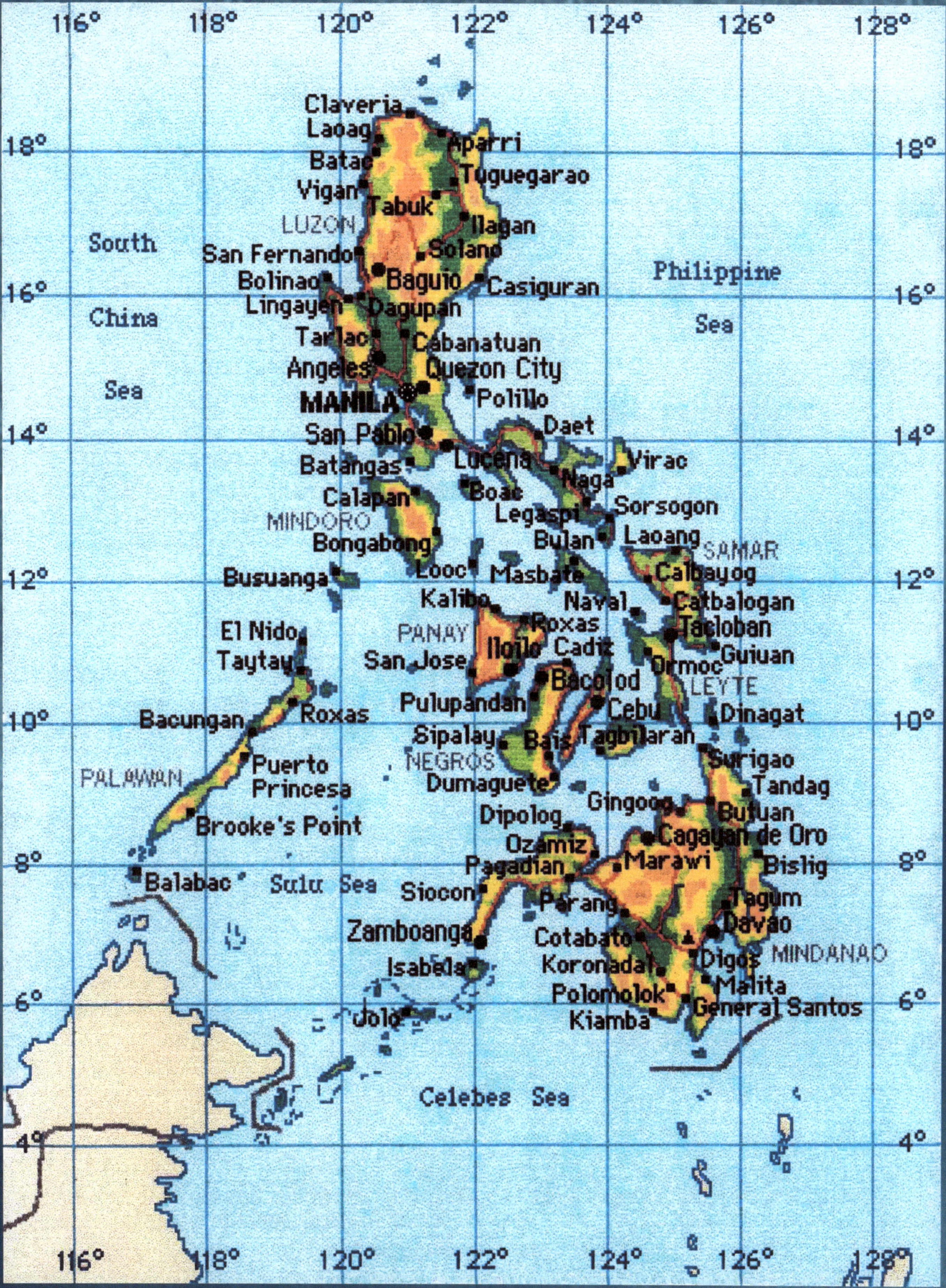
116°
118°
120°
122°
124°
126°
128°
18°
16°
14°
12°
10°
8°
6°
4°
South
China
Sea
Philippine
Sea
LUZON
Claveria
Laoag
Aparri
Batac
Tuguegarao
Vigan
Tabuk
Ilagan
San Fernando
Solano
Bolinao
Baguio
Casiguran
Lingayen
Dagupan
Tarlac
Cabanatuan
Angeles
Quezon City
MANILA
Polillo
San Pablo
Daet
Batangas
Lucena
Virac
Boac
Naga
Calapan
Sorsogon
MINDORO
Legaspi
Bongabong
Bulan
Laoang
SAMAR
Busuanga
Looc
Masbate
Calbayog
Kalibo
Naval
Catbalogan
El Nido
PANAY
Roxas
Tacloban
Taytay
San Jose
Iloilo
Cadiz
Ormoc
Guiuan
Bacolod
LEYTE
Pulupandan
Cebu
Dinagat
Bacungan
Roxas
Sipalay
Bais
Tagbilaran
Surigao
PALAWAN
Puerto
Princesa
NEGROS
Dumaguete
Tandag
Gingoog
Butuan
Brooke's Point
Dipolog
Cagayan de Oro
Ozamiz
Marawi
Bislig
Pagadian
Balabac
Sulu Sea
Siocon
Parang
Tagum
Zamboanga
Davao
Cotabato
Digos
MINDANAO
Isabela
Koronadal
Malita
Polomolok
General Santos
Jolo
Kiamba
Celebes Sea

Why Moroland Books:

After many adventurous weekends searching through gun shows, antique stores, antique shows, flea markets, estate sales, and other odd places collecting edged weapons, artifacts, and books about them, it was decided that Moroland Pictorial Publications would make a series of pictorial books. The intent of the writers was to make books that show a pictorial selection of edged weapons and artifacts to be shared with family, friends, the curious at heart and fellow collectors. These books were written for the experienced as well as the beginning collector in mind.

Book Style:

This style of book was chosen so the cost could be kept reasonable enough for anyone to afford collecting these books, even if collecting the items inside of them were out of their financial ability. The description pages simple format was chosen for easy reference and comparison. Full color photo like pages were decided upon to show more details and give an accurate representation of the coloration of these artifacts. The Little Extras section of these books was included to give the reader a few more interesting pieces of imformation about the people whose hard work created these artifacts.

Buying Tips:

Here are a few tips from experienced collectors of the most important things to remember when collecting. Antique values can fluctuate dramatically. Only collect items that you personally like. If it interest you and is in an acceptable condition, then buy it at that time. Most people pass up this opportunity to purchase and when they return the item is gone. Closely inspect what interest you to see if it is damaged, broken, or has missing pieces. As a rule, values decline when condition declines. Always bring enough cash to purchase the item when you first see it, If that is not possible try to bargain a payment plan including location and time. As a final tip, it is a good idea to write the details of your agreement down and have both parties sign it to avoid conflict later.

Care and repair of carved wood:

It is a good idea to avoid extreme temperatures or humidity when storing wooden artifacts. Always handle carved wooden artifacts with care since age and composition can make them very delicate. Many people use linseed oil or a protective coating of stain to protect their artifacts. Care should be taken to select the appropriate matching stain as to not change the coloration of the artifact. Get professional help when needed.

Hobby:

This hobby is a very interesting and exciting pastime for the young and old alike. What ever your motivation for collecting is, the find is well worth the excitement of the hunt. You will discover that this book is a valuable field guide while on the hunt for any art or artifacts from Moroland or its neighbors.

INTRODUCTION

GENERAL INFORMATION:

This book is intended to show a sample of various artistic objects from in and around the Philippines. This area of islands and various countries is what we respectfully call Moroland. The name Moroland actually stands for the Moro tribes of the Philippine Islands. The Philippine tribes are some of the most vicious warriors on the face of the earth as well as skilled craftsmen. The people of Moroland are very religious, respectful, and a traditional family oriented society. Their art reflects their dedication to their values and resourcefulness.

There are many types and varieties of artifacts designed, carved, and manufactured by the Moro people. Most carved artifacts are replicas of live animals, humans, gods, historical figures, geometric patterns, or just natural beauty. Our pictorial books will cover some of the these artifacts. Each tribe, family, or master carver has designed their own variations or styles. They devised their own techniques to manufacture these items with the materials found in and around their homes and villages. The Moroland people are a resourceful people.

MOROLAND TRADITIONS:

The skills of their crafts are passed from family to family and generation to generation by the tradition of the master craftsman. These traditions can be traced back many centuries. A young child starts out being taught through years of repetition how to carve the very roughest of the first cuts, sanding, and painting to the wood. As their skills develop they are given training in the more advanced carving or shaping of the intricate details of the artifacts. After many more years of waiting they become the master carvers assistant or apprentice. The apprentices of the master carver will devote all their time and sacrifice much of their lives to gain the well deserved knowledge and title of Master Carver. Traditionally the men will do the carving and women and children will do the sanding and painting of the art. The family lives their life around traditional manufacturing of carved artifacts and their ability to sell them to their customers or tourists.

LOST ART:

Moroland's material resources are being depleted. It has driven up the cost of the materials used to create the artifacts. Resulting in many of these skilled craftmen loosing their lively hood. Western civilizations values and technology are causing the young people to not have a desire to continue in their strong family traditions or manufacturing techniques. The next generation of potential master carvers are being driven to look for employment opportunities in different lines of work. This is causing Moroland's traditional art manufacturing to become a lost art. These trends have caused the values of old or well preserved artifacts to rise in price.

ARTIFACTS

of

MOROLAND MUSEUM

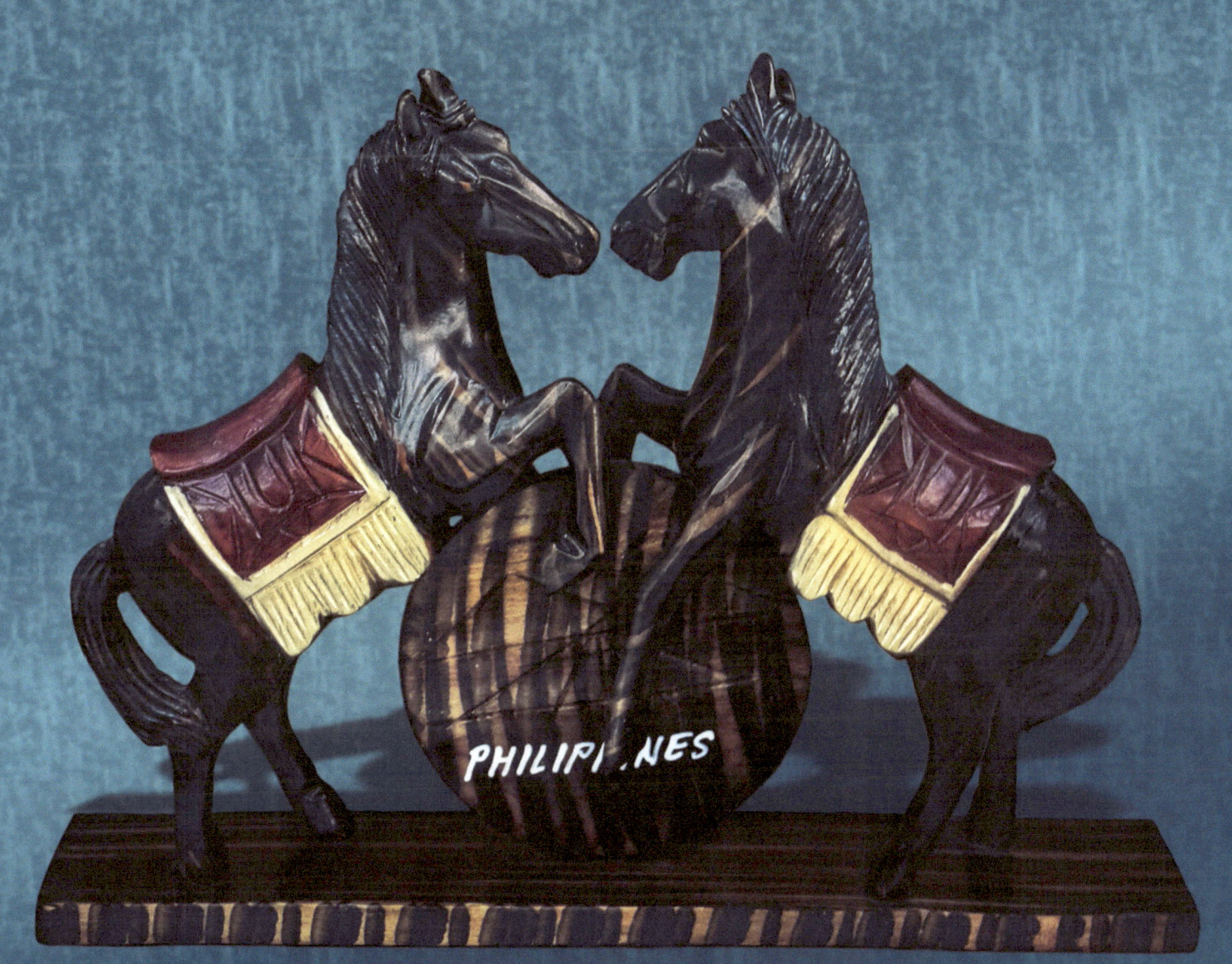

ARTIFACTS of MOROLAND MUSEUM
ARTIFACT DESCRIPTION

DESCRIPTION: #01 Philippine Mustang Stallions

LENGTH: 16 inches

WIDTH: 4 inches

HEIGHT: 12 inches

COMPOSITION: Hard Stained Wood, Gold Paint

COLOR: Brown, Tan, Gold, Red, Yellow, White, Black

COMMENTS: Spanish Stallions

LOCATION OF FIND: Manila Craft Market

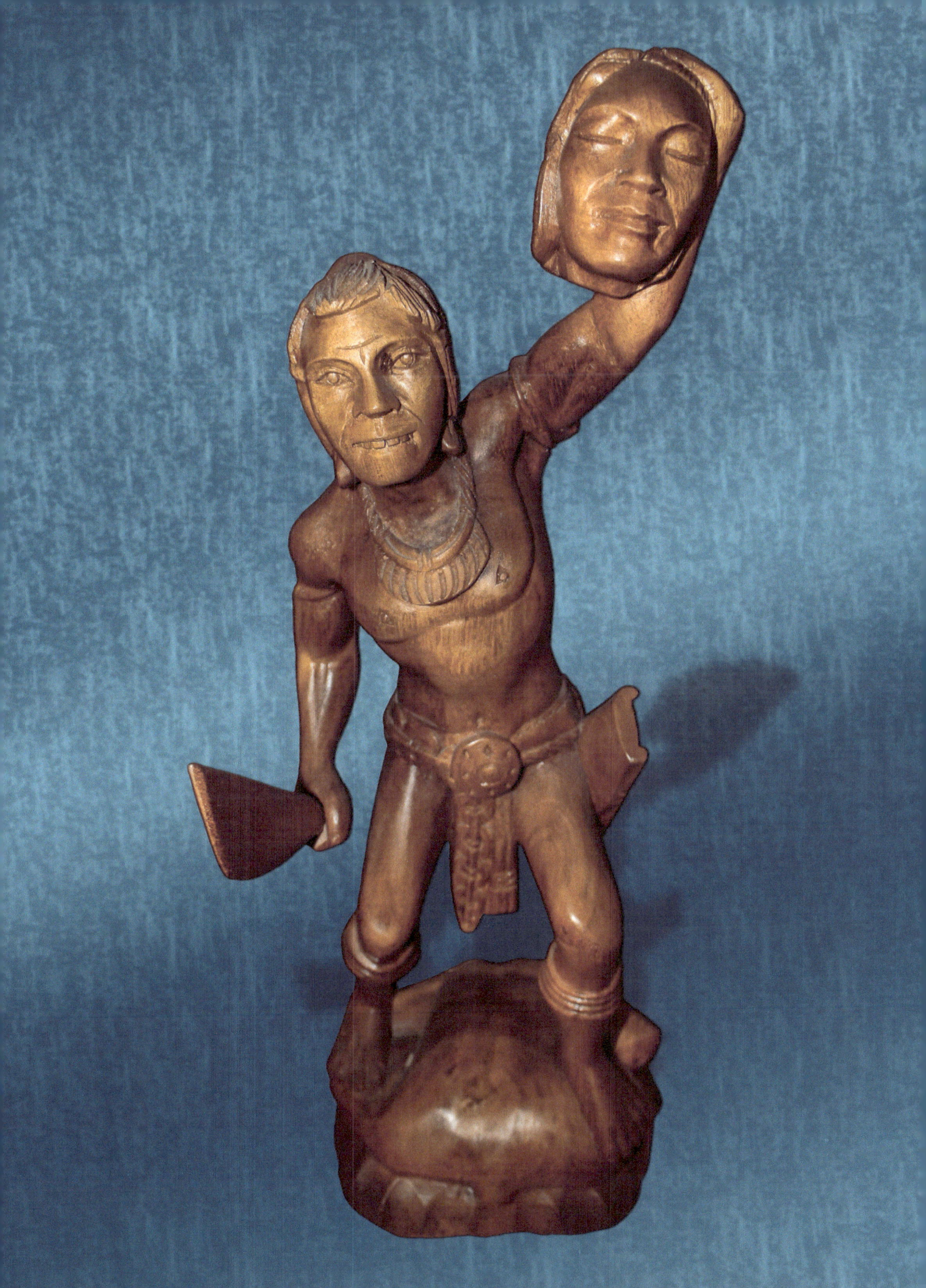

ARTIFACTS of MOROLAND MUSEUM

ARTIFACT DESCRIPTION

DESCRIPTION: #02 Igorot Headhunter

LENGTH: 7 inches

WIDTH: 6 inches

HEIGHT: 24 inches

COMPOSITION: Wood

COLOR: Light Brown, Cream

COMMENTS: Old, nice detailed craftsmanship

LOCATION OF FIND: Flea Market

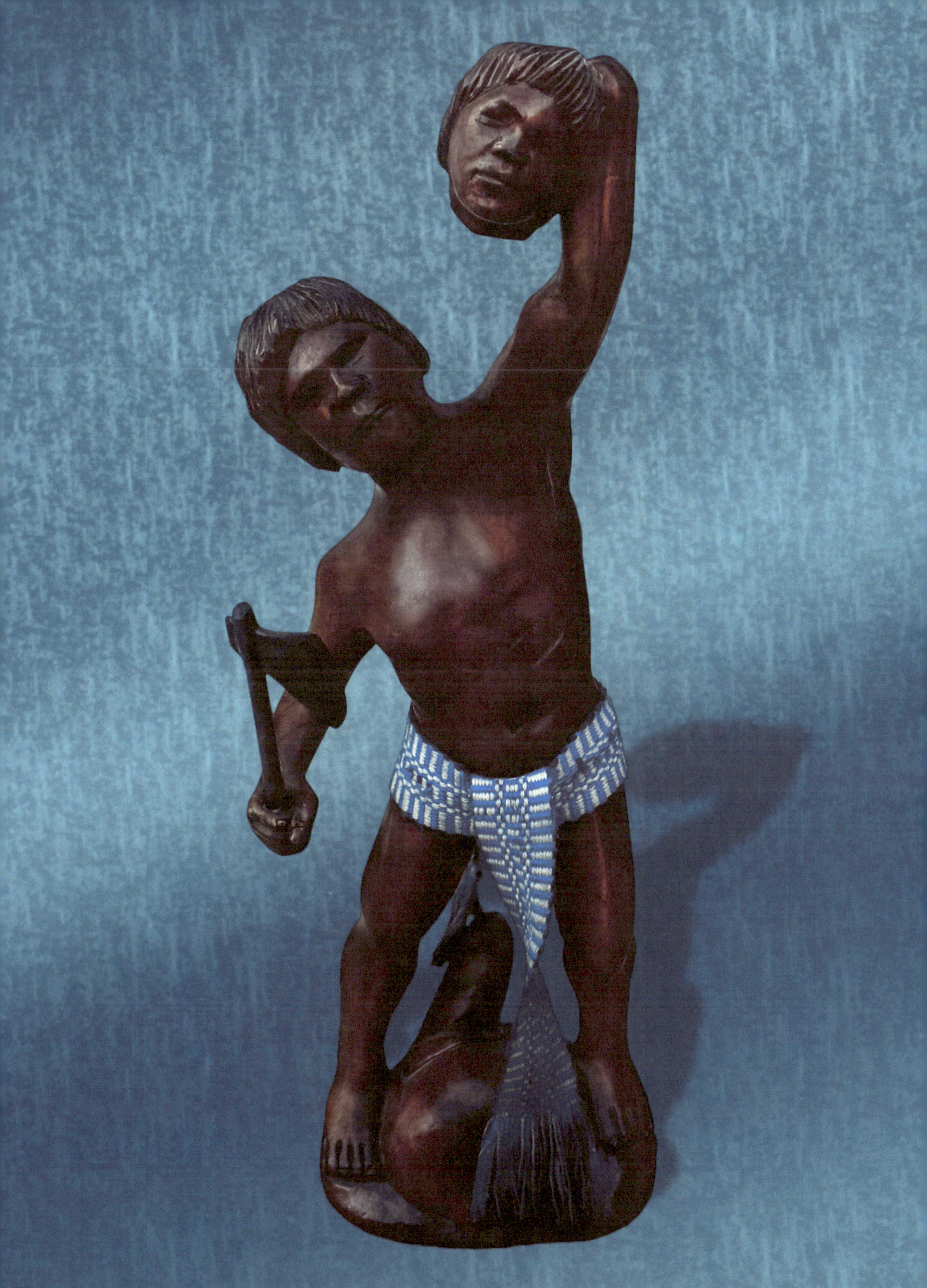

ARTIFACT DESCRIPTION

DESCRIPTION: #03 Igorot Headhunter

LENGTH: 6 inches

WIDTH: 7 inches

HEIGHT: 26 inches

COMPOSITION: Wood, Cloth

COLOR: Dark Brown, White, Blue

COMMENTS: Traditional cloth garment. Has a battle axe in hand.

LOCATION OF FIND: Manila Craft Market

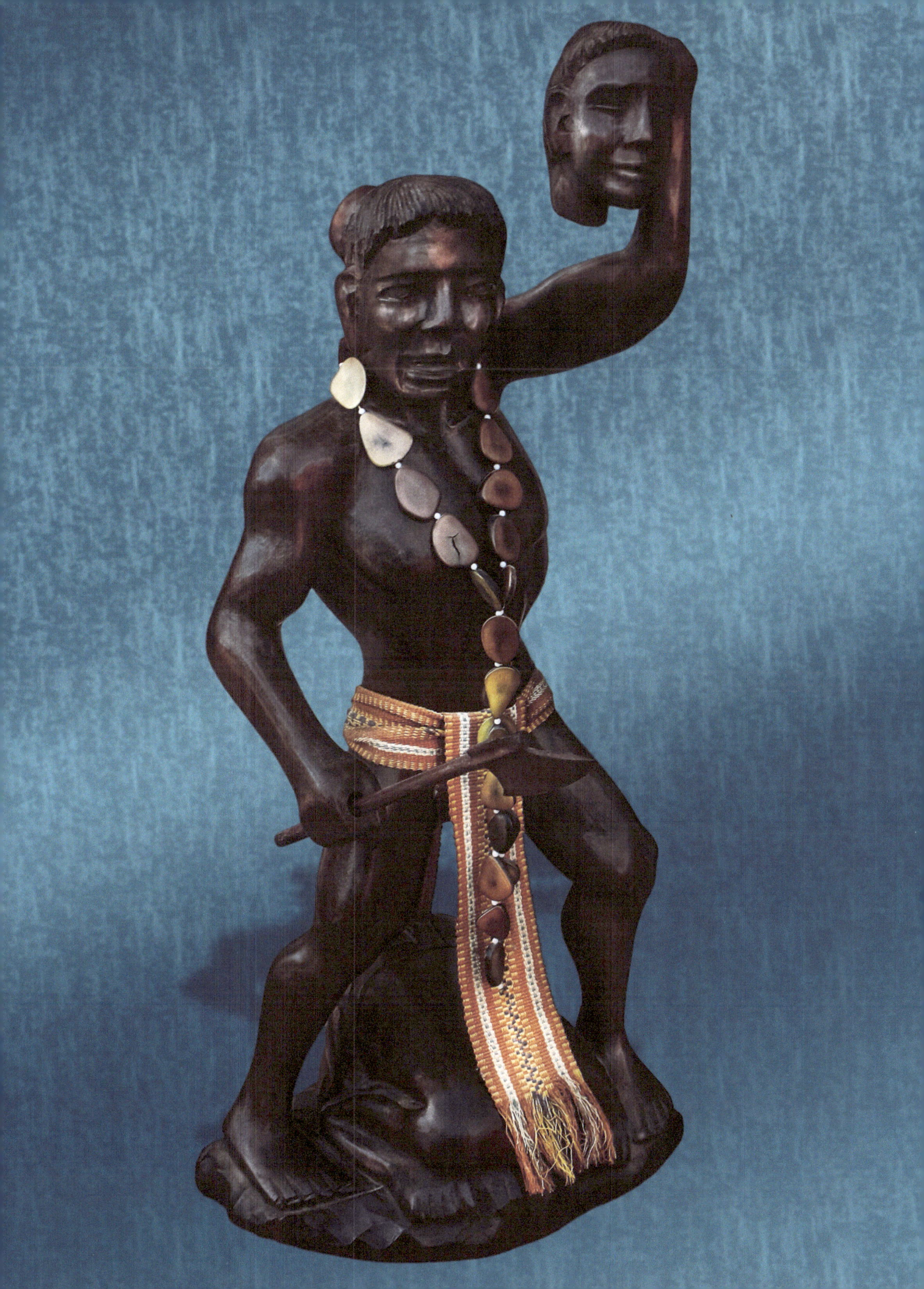

ARTIFACT DESCRIPTION

DESCRIPTION: #04 Igorot Headhunter

LENGTH: 9 inches

WIDTH: 8 inches

HEIGHT: 28 inches

COMPOSITION: Wood, Cloth, Banana Nut Wood, Metal, Rattan Wrap

COLOR: Dark Brown, Orange, Yellow, White, Black, Silver

COMMENTS: Battle Axe in hand and Bolo in traditional cloth garment. His necklace is made of Banana Nut wood beads.

LOCATION OF FIND: Antique Store

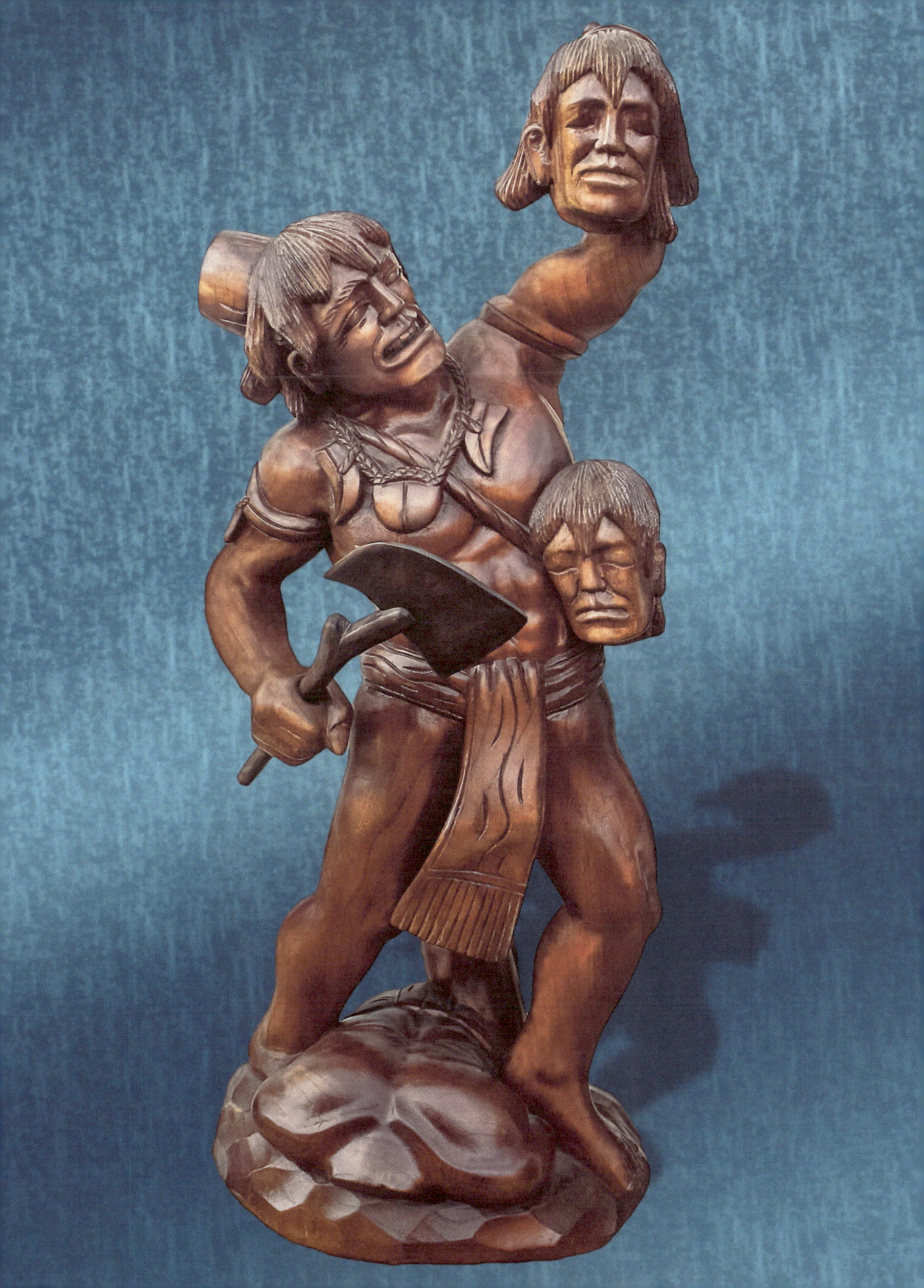

ARTIFACT DESCRIPTION

DESCRIPTION: #05 Igorot Headhunter

LENGTH: 8 inches

WIDTH: 9 inches

HEIGHT: 32 inches

COMPOSITION: Wood, Metal

COLOR: Brown, Gray

COMMENTS: Very detailed Carving. Has two detached heads.

LOCATION OF FIND: Manila Craft Market

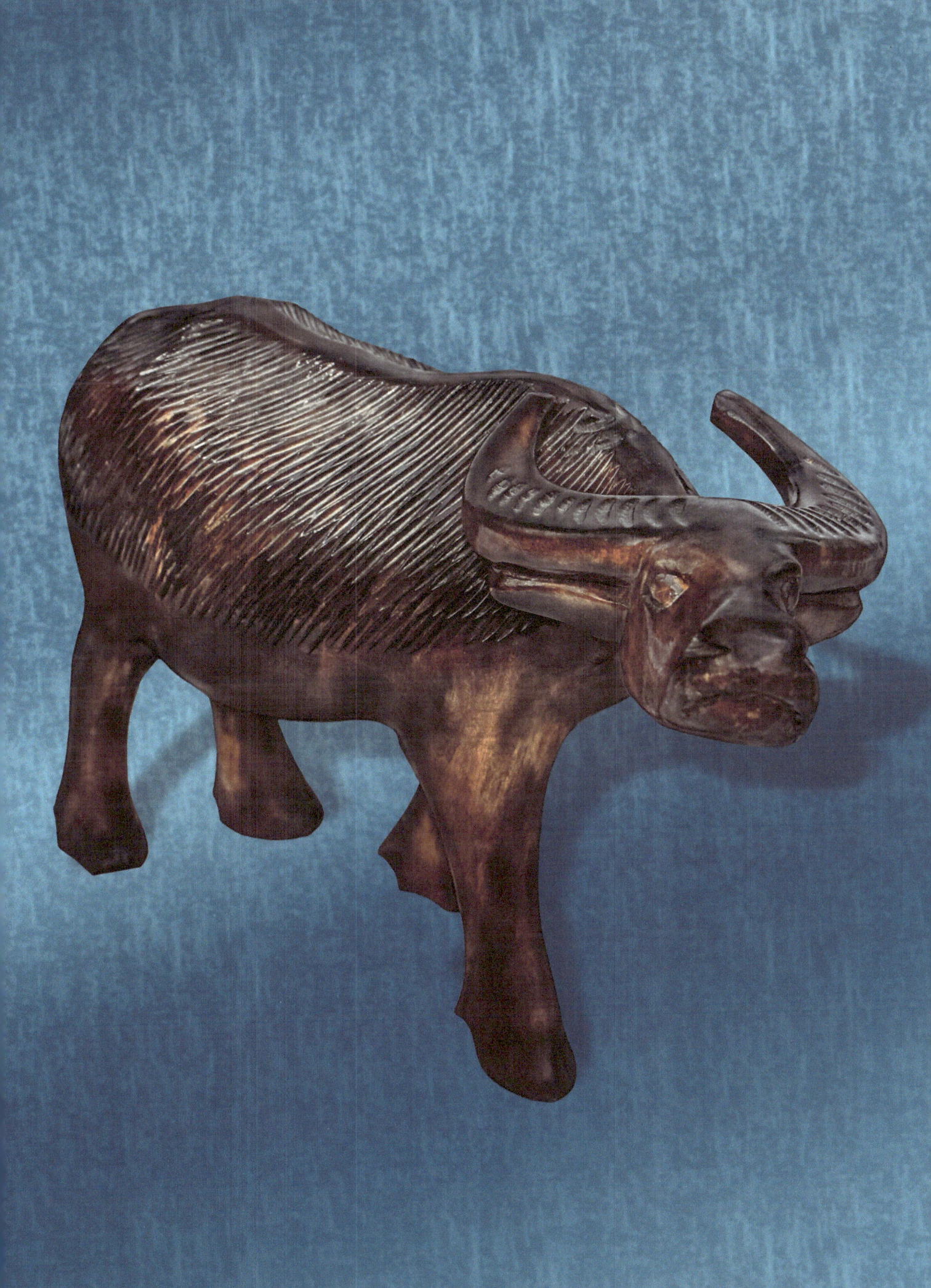

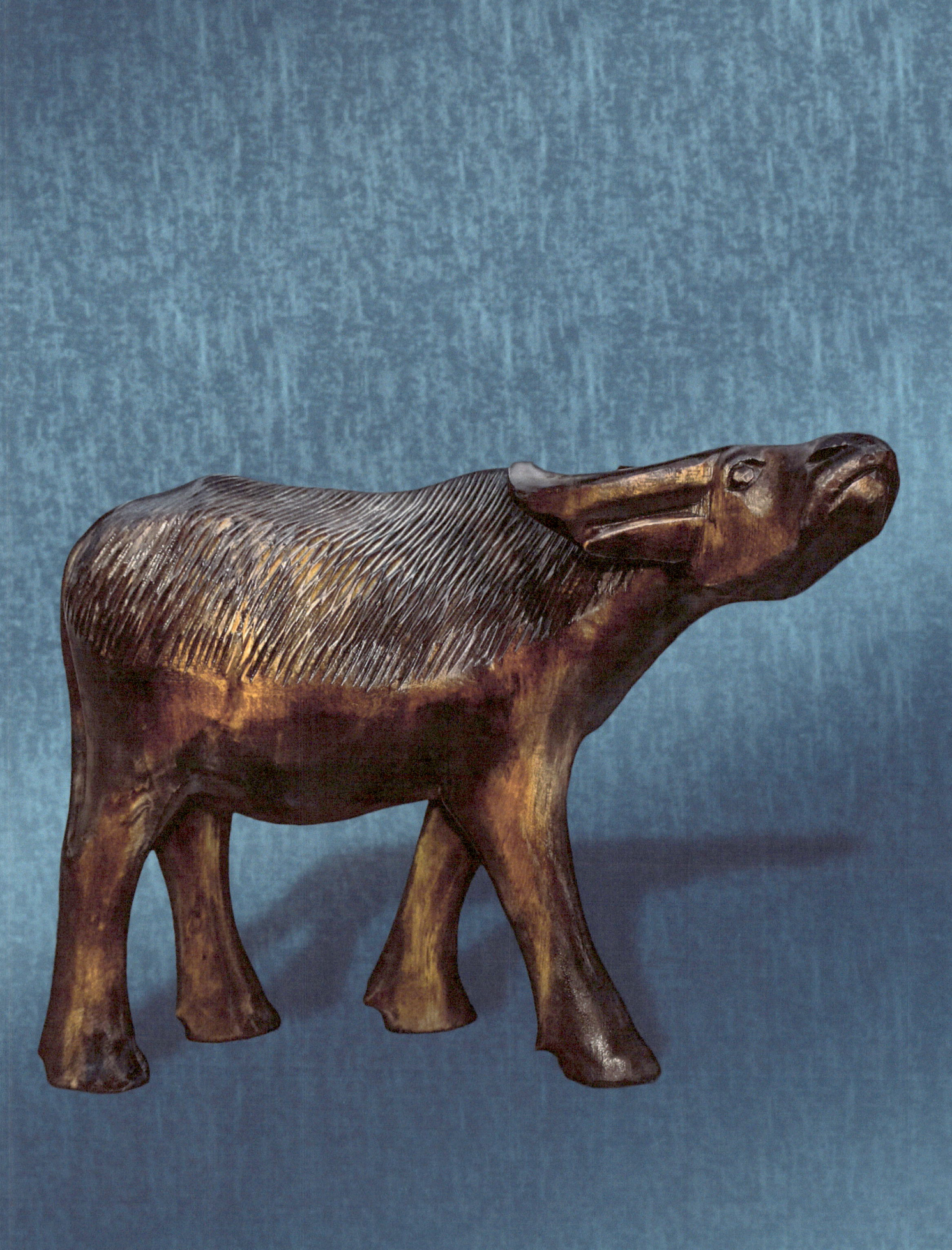

ARTIFACT DESCRIPTION

DESCRIPTION: #06 Water Buffalo

LENGTH: 13 inches

WIDTH: 4 inches

HEIGHT: 10 inches

COMPOSITION: Wood

COLOR: Dark Brown

COMMENTS: Intricately carved details. Heavy.

LOCATION OF FIND: Manila Craft Market

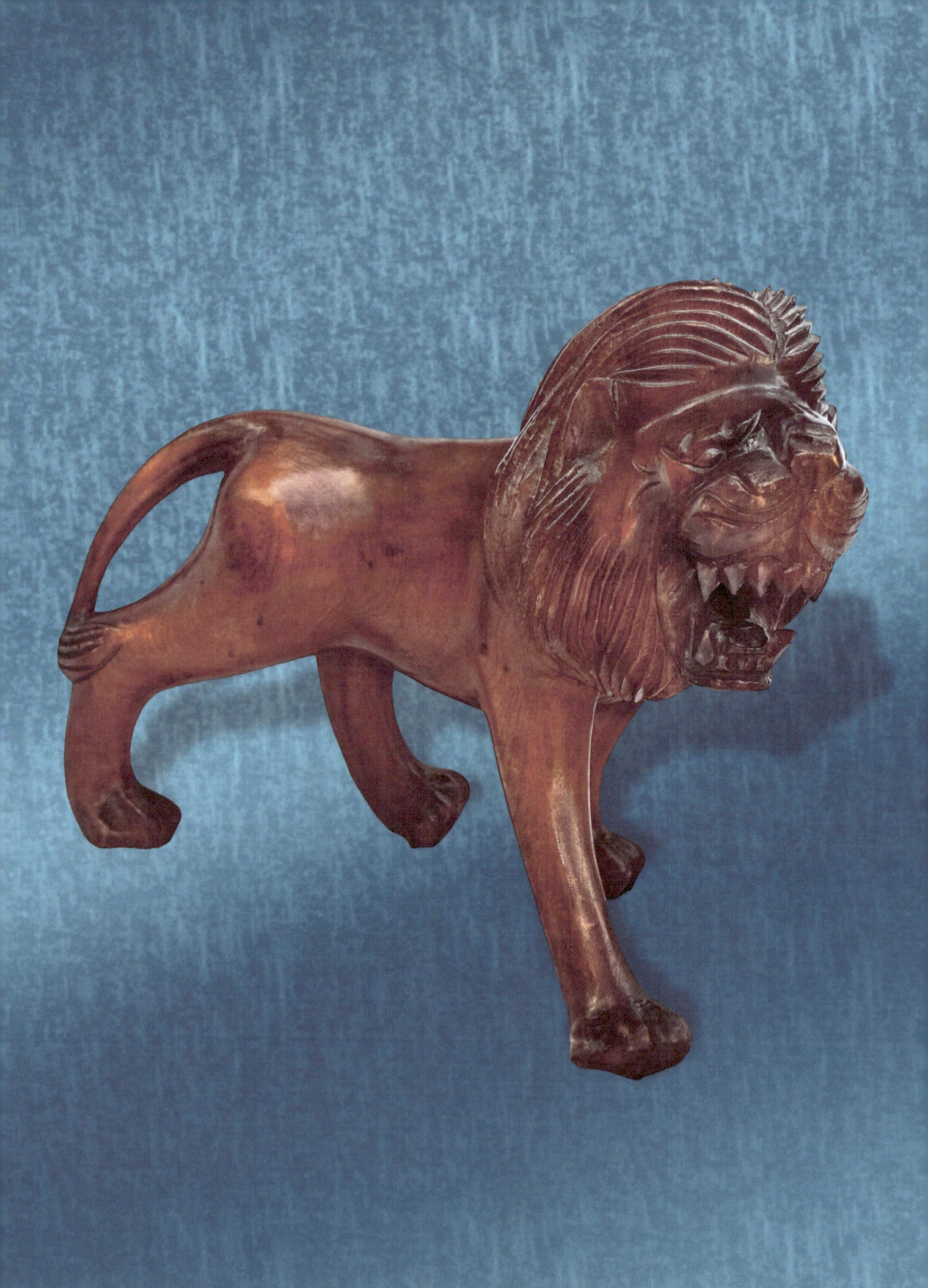

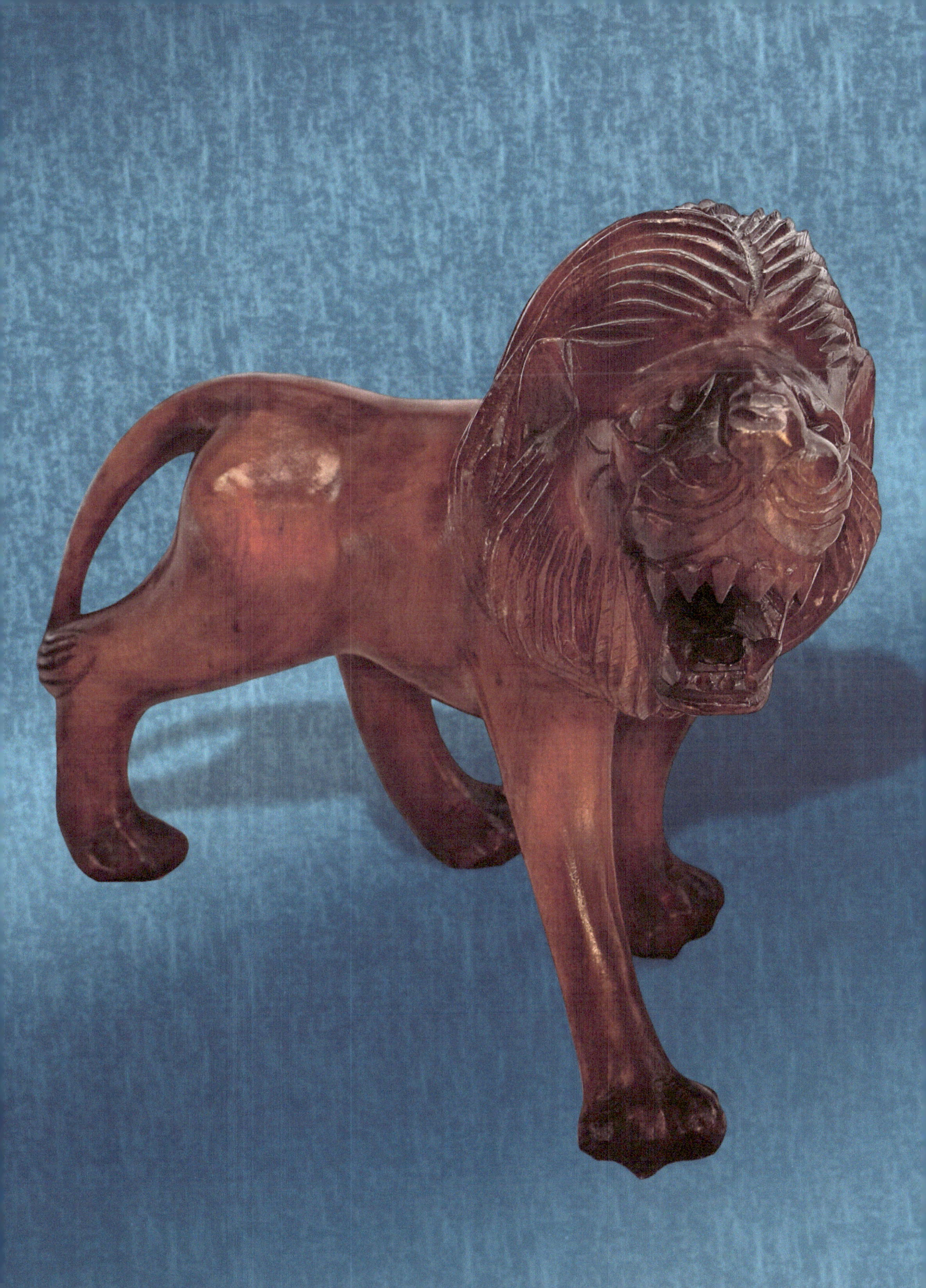

ARTIFACT DESCRIPTION

DESCRIPTION: #07 Lion

LENGTH: __17 inches__

WIDTH: __4 inches__

HEIGHT: __10 inches__

COMPOSITION: ___Wood___

COLOR: __Brown__

COMMENTS: ___Semi-detailed carved wood.___

LOCATION OF FIND: ___Manila Craft Market__

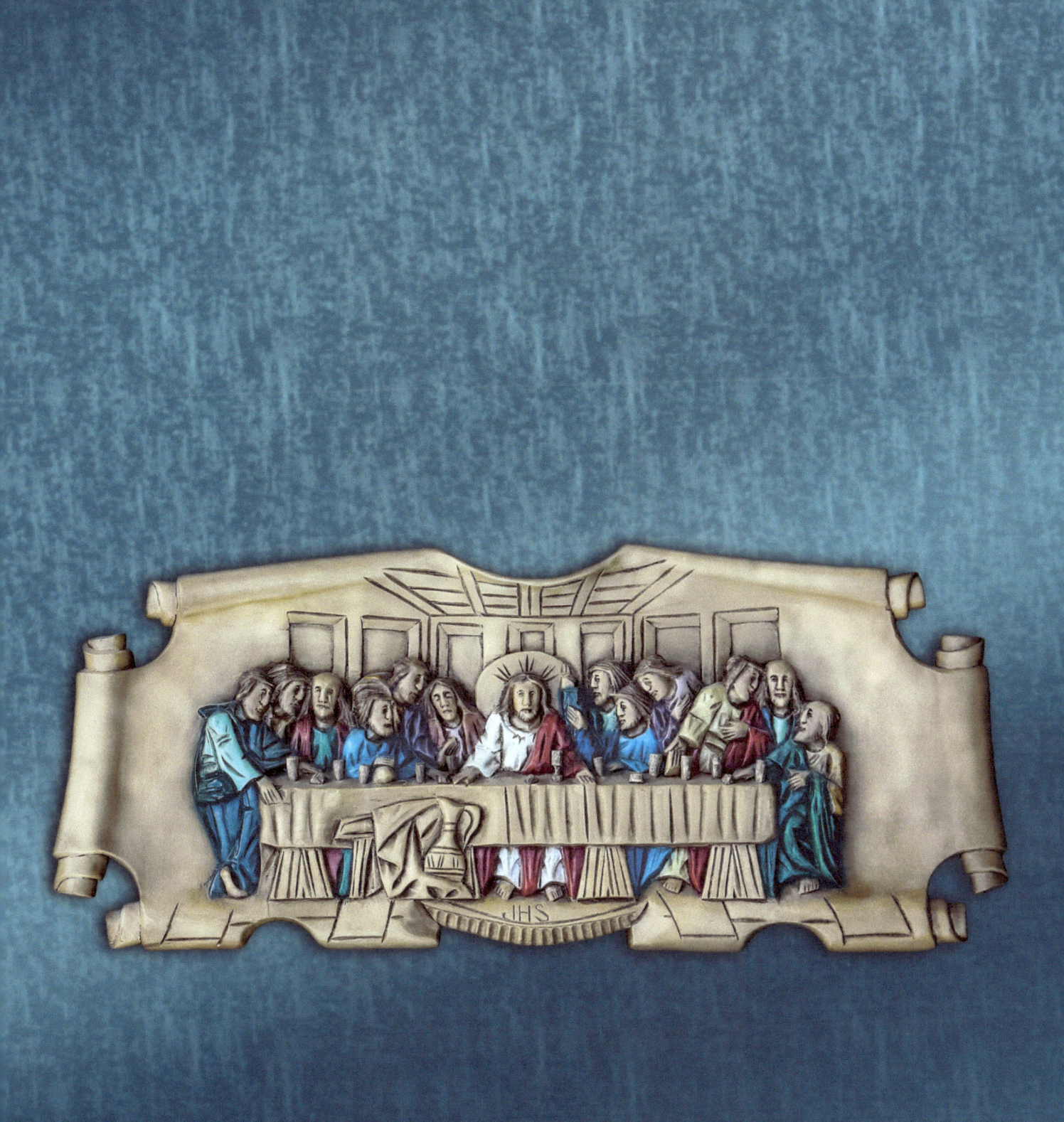

ARTIFACT DESCRIPTION

DESCRIPTION: #08 Last Supper Plaque

LENGTH: 24 inches

WIDTH: 10 inches

HEIGHT: 1 1/2 inches

COMPOSITION: Wood, Gold, Paint

COLOR: Brown, Dark Brown, Gold, White, Red, Yellow, Light Green
              Blue, Aqua, Black, Tan

COMMENTS: Very detailed carving. Nicely hand painted.

LOCATION OF FIND: Manila Craft Market

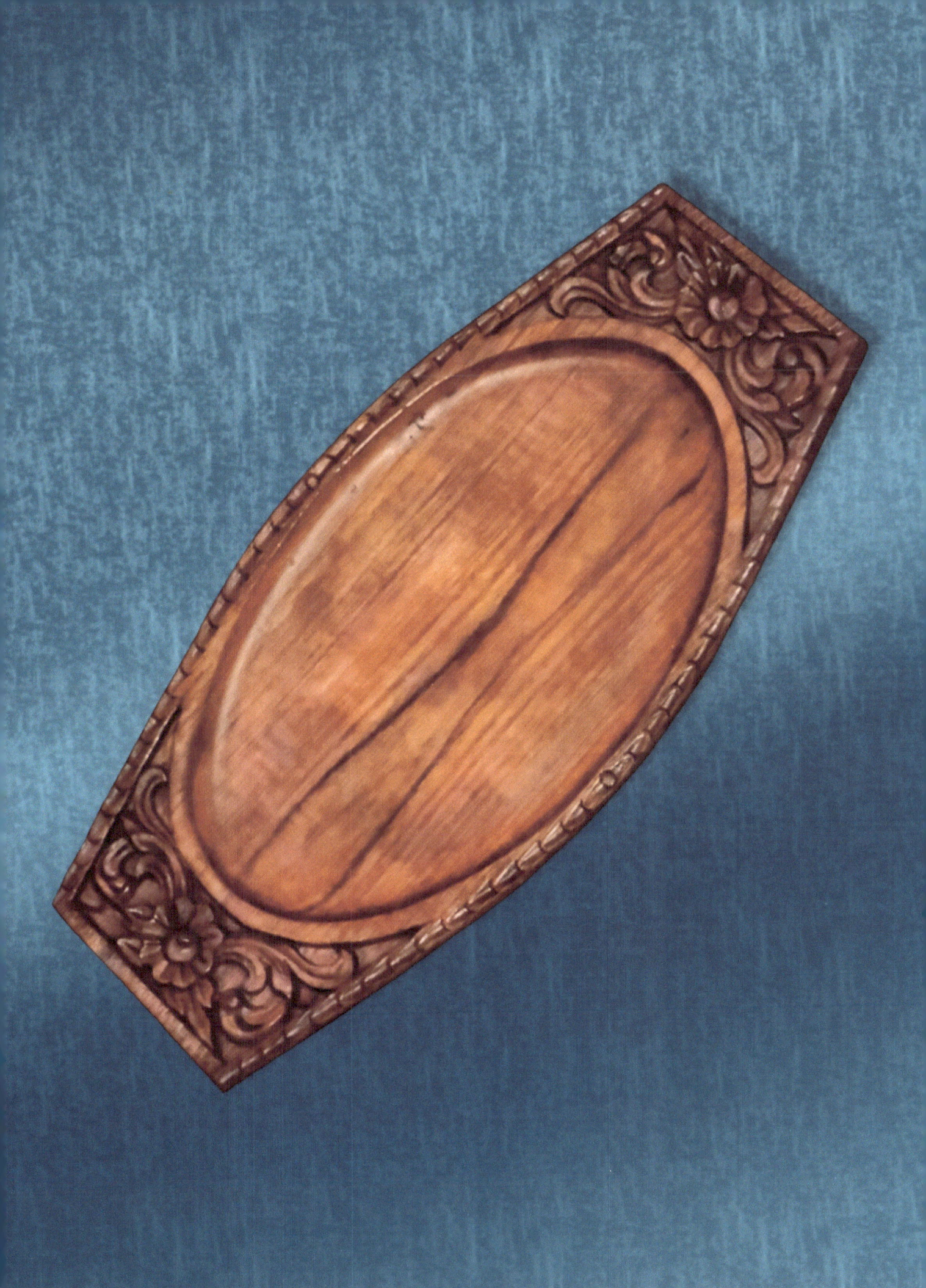

ARTIFACT DESCRIPTION

DESCRIPTION: #09 Serving Platter

LENGTH: 26 inches

WIDTH: 12 inches

HEIGHT: 1 inch

COMPOSITION: Wood

COLOR: Brown

COMMENTS: Nice floral pattern carving.

LOCATION OF FIND: Antique Store

28

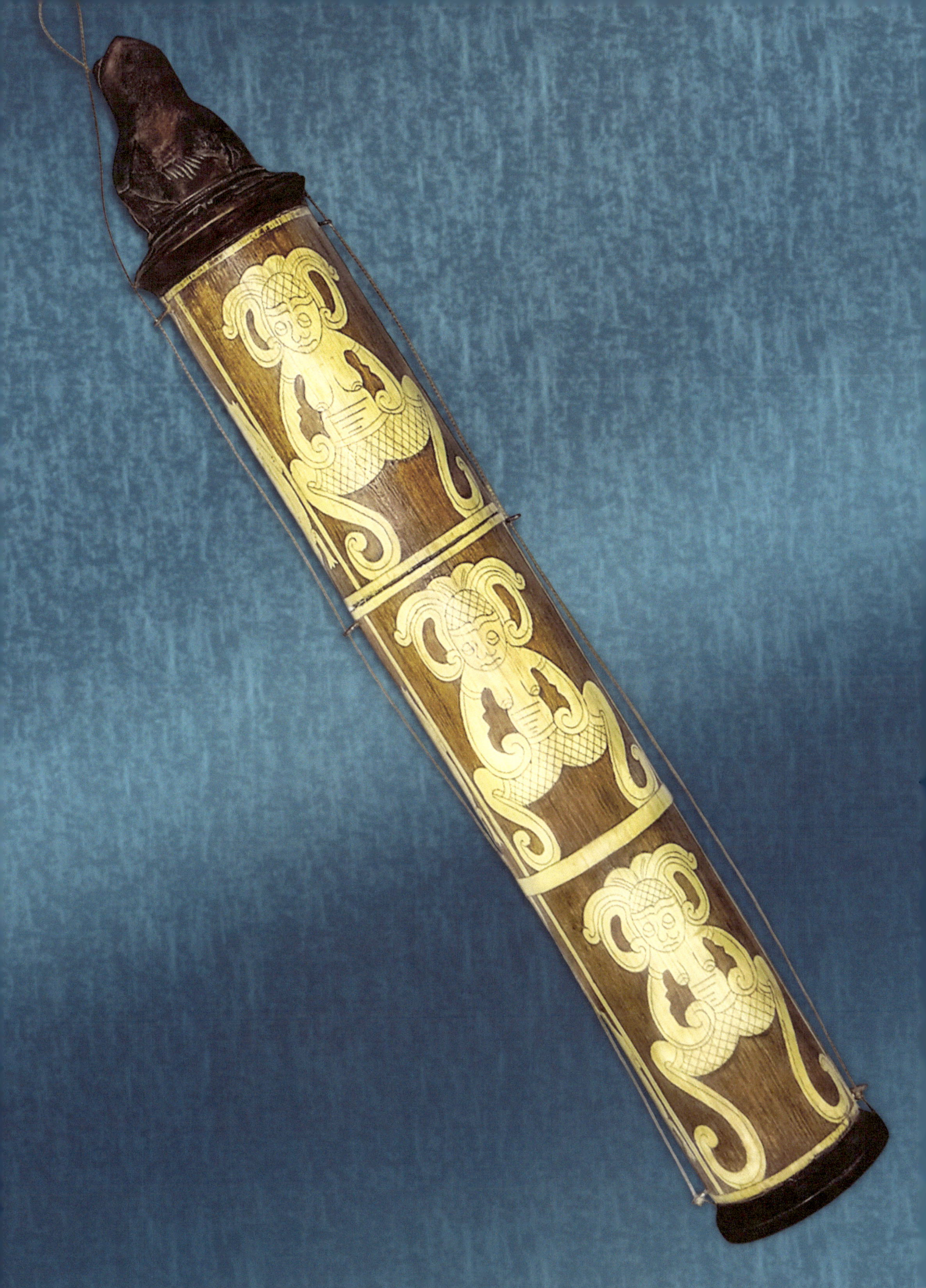

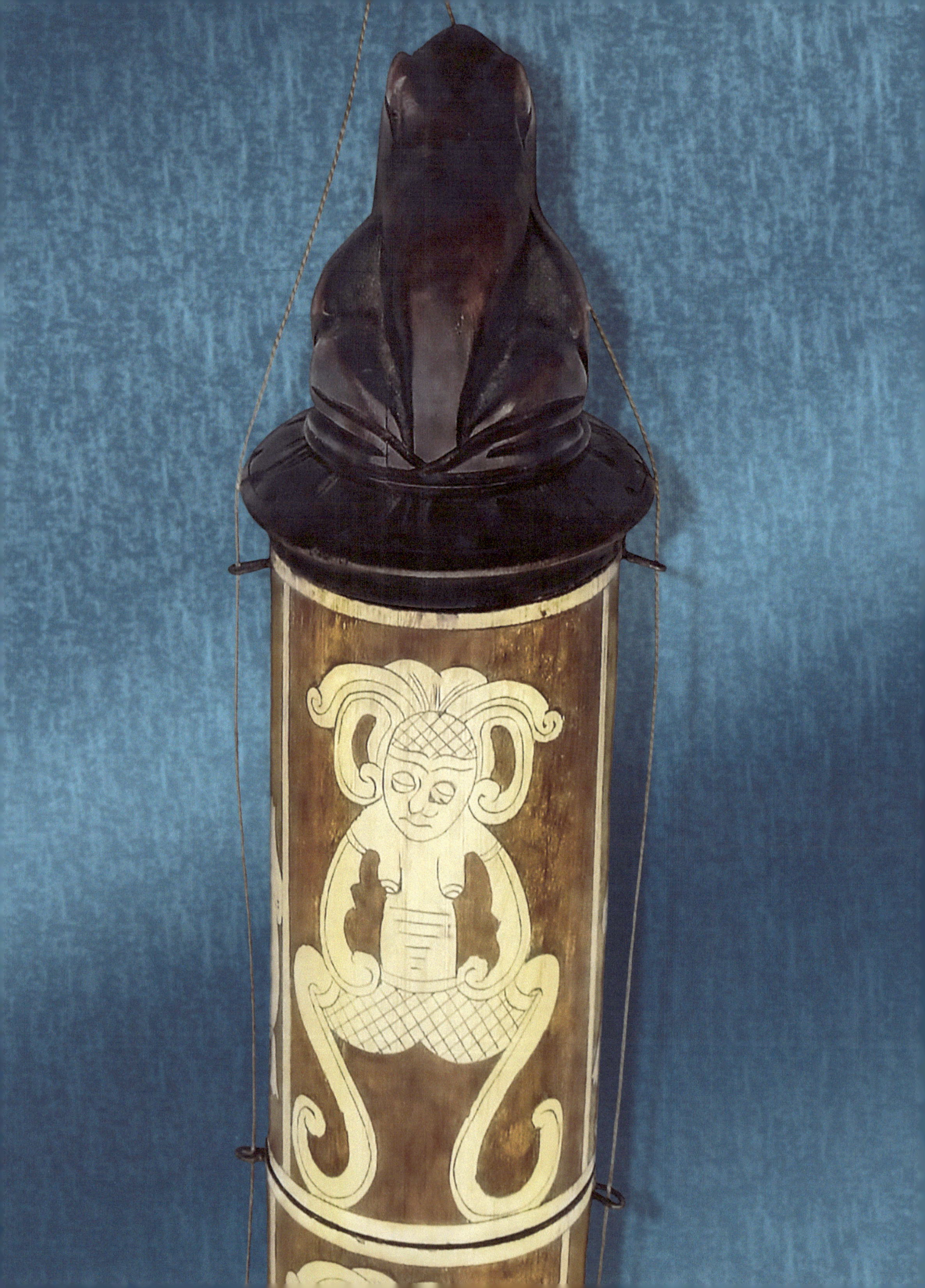

ARTIFACT DESCRIPTION

DESCRIPTION: #10 Indonesian Letter Carrier

LENGTH: 18 inches

WIDTH: 3 inches

HEIGHT: 3 inches

COMPOSITION: Wood, Bamboo, Rope

COLOR: Brown, Tan

COMMENTS: Carved frog on top of the lid. Carved ladies on body of carrier.

LOCATION OF FIND: Antique Store

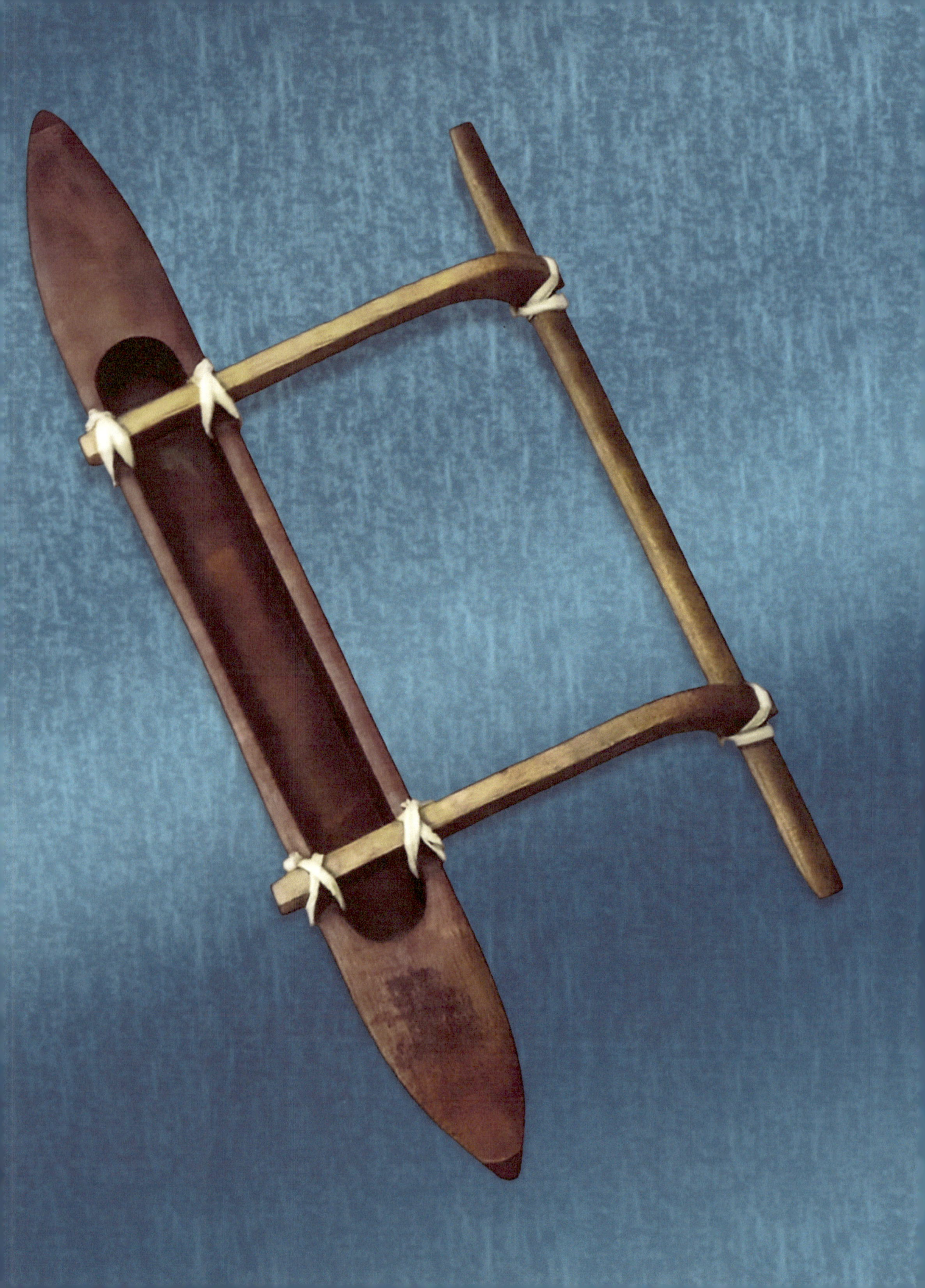

ARTIFACTS of MOROLAND MUSEUM
ARTIFACT DESCRIPTION

DESCRIPTION: #11 Igorot Canoe

LENGTH: 13 inches

WIDTH: 5 inches

HEIGHT: 1.5 inches

COMPOSITION: Wood, Rattan

COLOR: Brown, Tan

COMMENTS: Heavy

LOCATION OF FIND: Flea Market

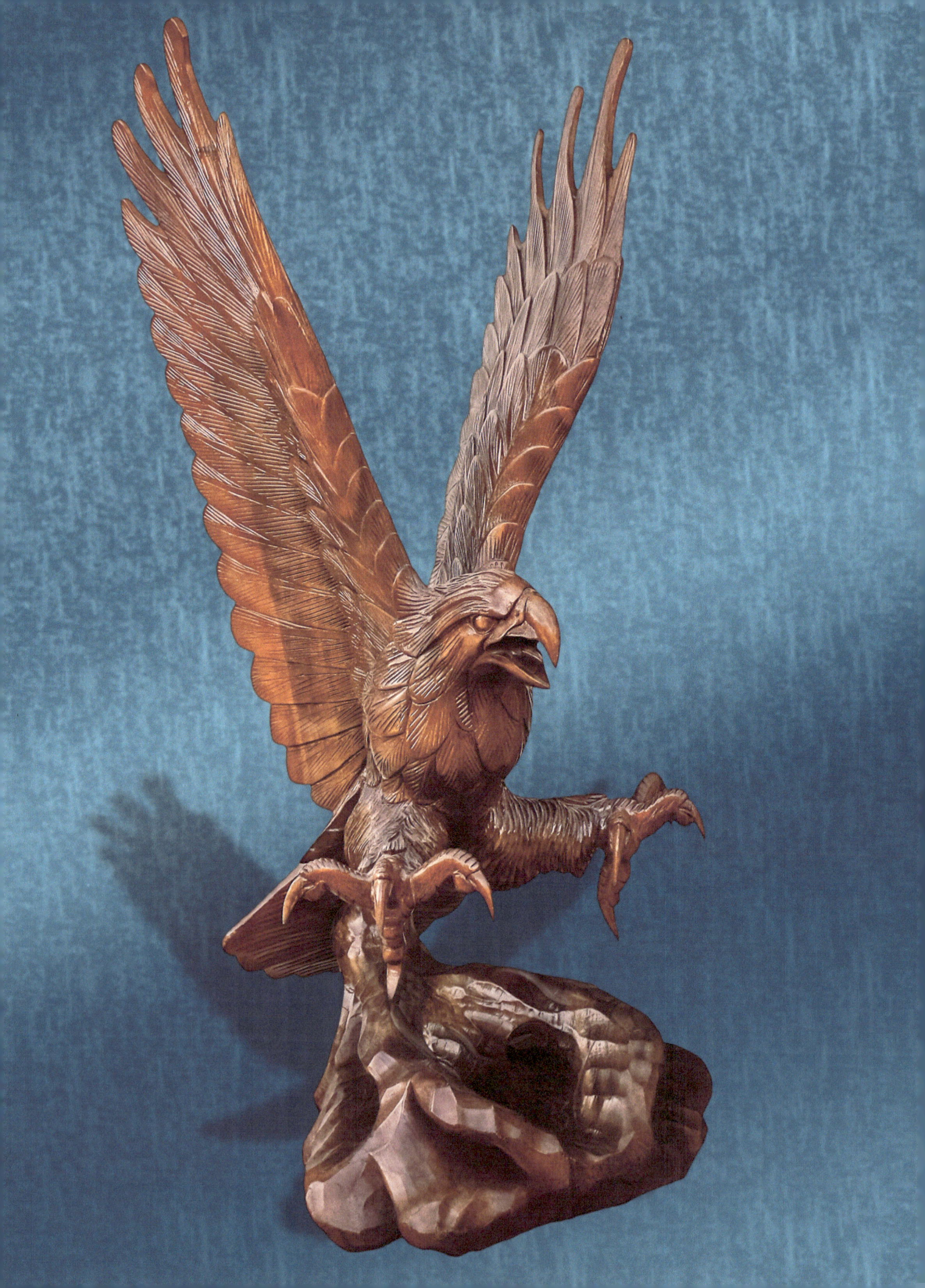

ARTIFACTS of MOROLAND MUSEUM
ARTIFACT DESCRIPTION

DESCRIPTION: #12 Philippine Golden Eagle

LENGTH: 15 inches

WIDTH: 16 inches

HEIGHT: 37 inches

COMPOSITION: Wood

COLOR: Brown

COMMENTS: very detailed carving

LOCATION OF FIND: Manila Craft Market

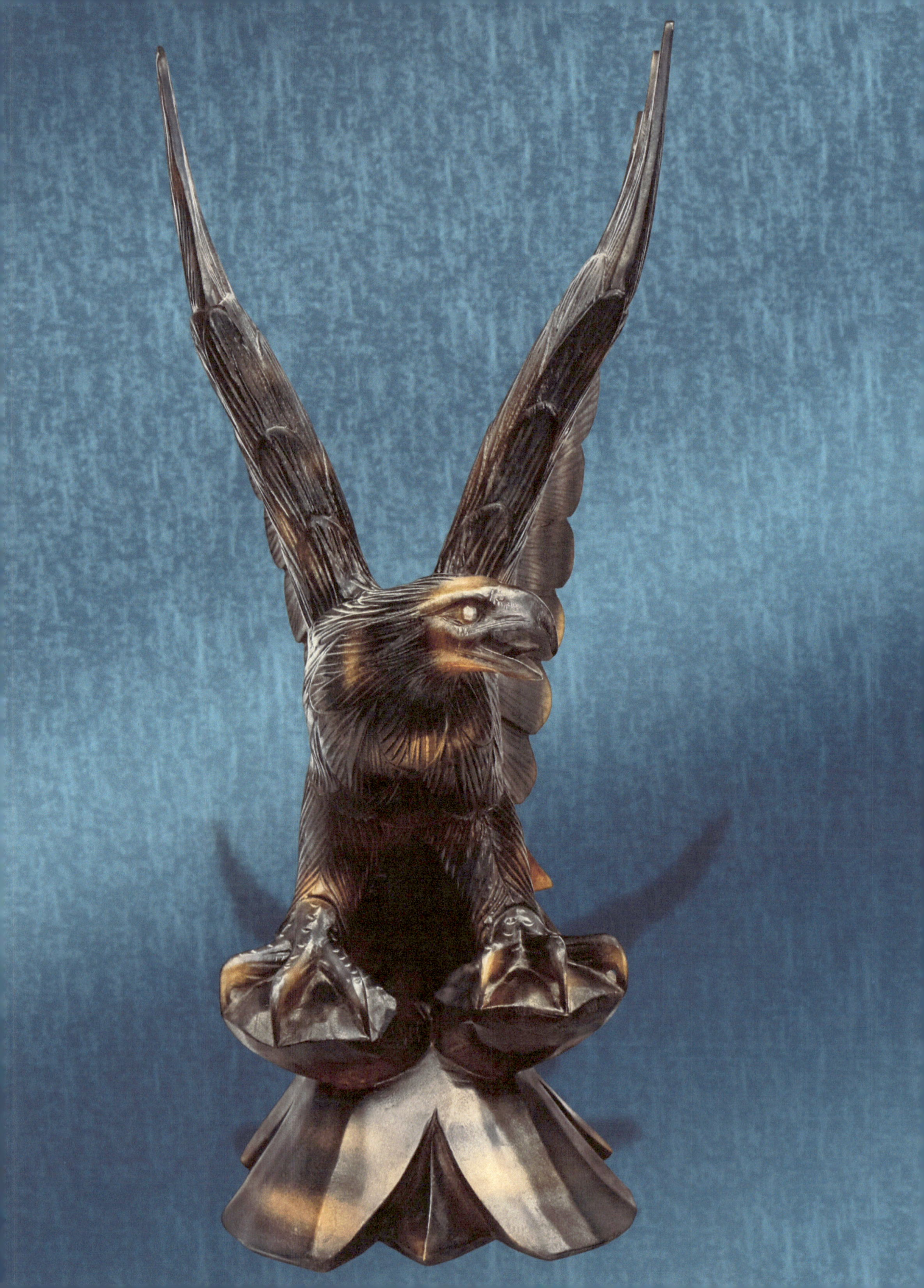

ARTIFACT DESCRIPTION

DESCRIPTION: #13 Philippine Golden Eagle

LENGTH: 10 inches

WIDTH: 10 inches

HEIGHT: 26 inches

COMPOSITION: Wood

COLOR: Black and Brown

COMMENTS: very detailed carving

LOCATION OF FIND: Manila Craft Market

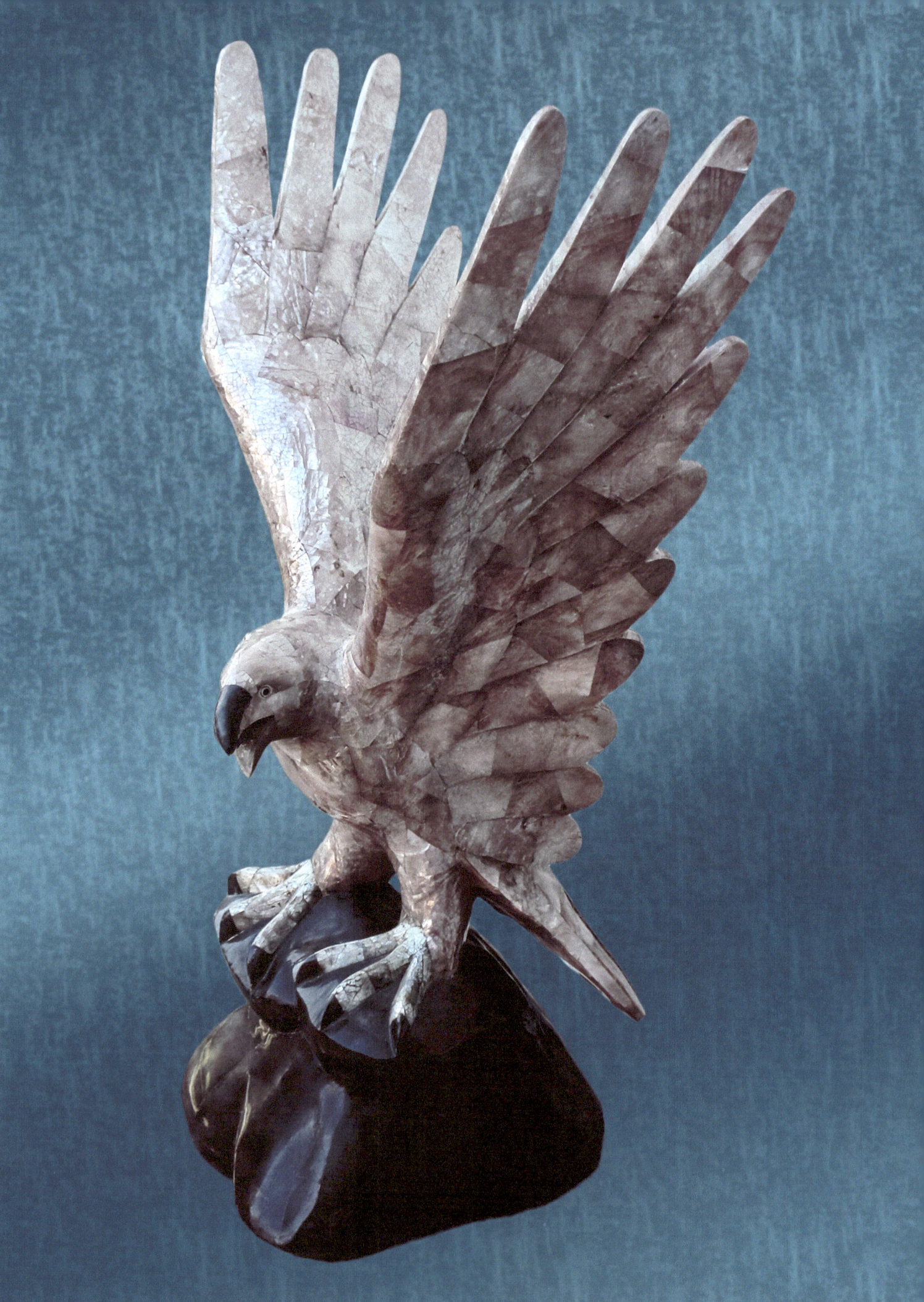

ARTIFACT DESCRIPTION

DESCRIPTION: #14 Philippine Golden Eagle

LENGTH: 15 inches

WIDTH: 14 inches

HEIGHT: 32 inches

COMPOSITION: Wood

COLOR: Black, Silver and Brown

COMMENTS: Three different kinds of very detailed Mother of Pearl shell inlay were used in the manufacture of this artifact . Black Lip shell on the beak and claws, Brown (Golden) Lip shell on the feathers and Silver Lip shell were used on the feet. These types of mother of Pearl are getting hard to find.

LOCATION OF FIND: Manila Craft Market

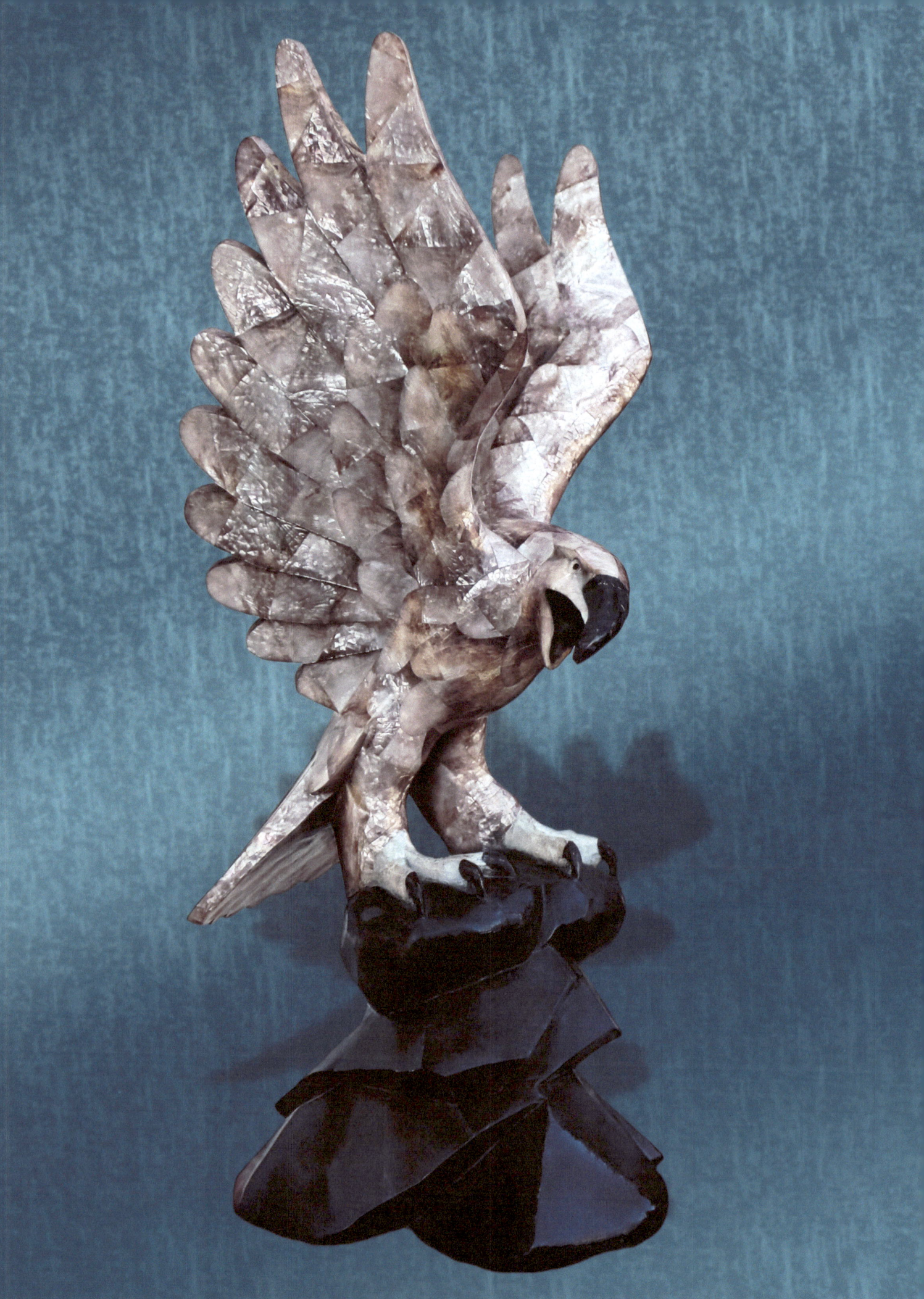

ARTIFACTS of MOROLAND MUSEUM
ARTIFACT DESCRIPTION

DESCRIPTION: #15 Philippine Golden Eagle

LENGTH: 14 inches

WIDTH: 15 inches

HEIGHT: 28 inches

COMPOSITION: Wood

COLOR: Black, Silver and Brown

COMMENTS: Three different kinds of very detailed Mother of Pearl shell inlay were used in the manufacture of this artifact . Black Lip shell on the beak and claws, Brown (Golden) Lip shell on the feathers and Silver Lip shell were used on the feet. These types of mother of Pearl are getting hard to find.

LOCATION OF FIND: Manila Craft Market

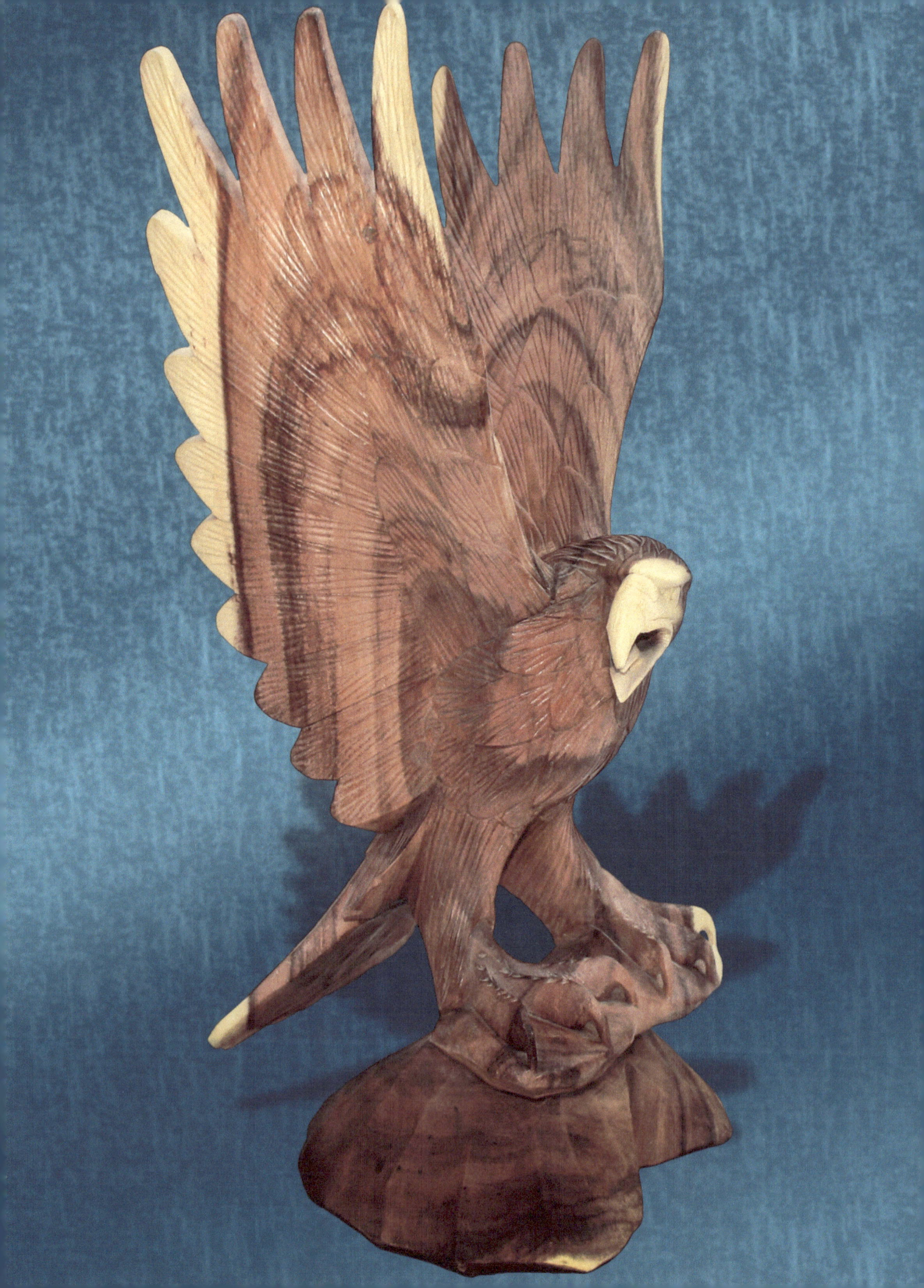

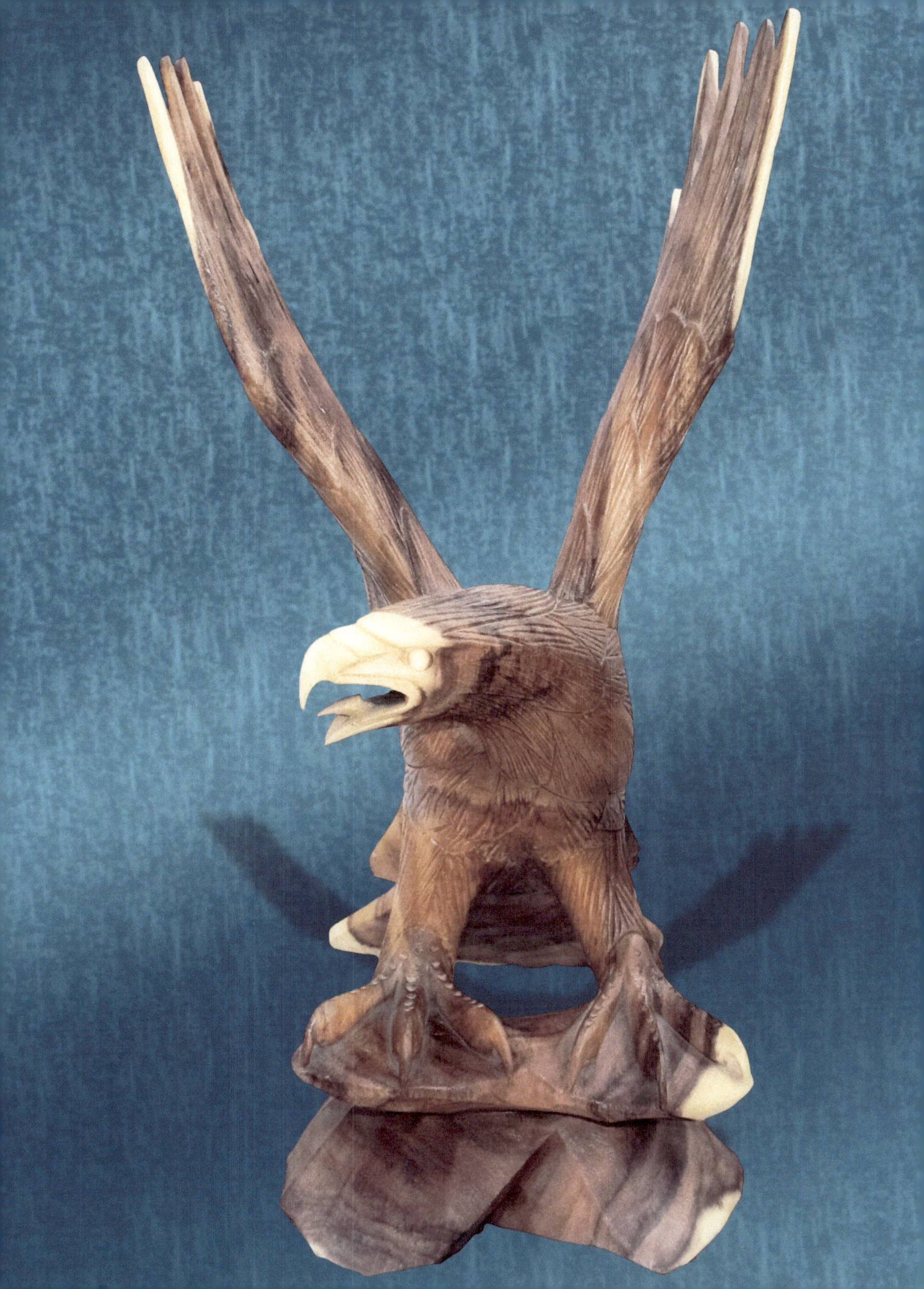

ARTIFACT DESCRIPTION

DESCRIPTION: #16 Philippine Golden Eagle

LENGTH: 12 inches

WIDTH: 12 inches

HEIGHT: 24 inches

COMPOSITION: Wood

COLOR: Brown, Cream, Black, Light Brown

COMMENTS: Excellent coloration. Intricate carved details.

LOCATION OF FIND: Manila Craft Market

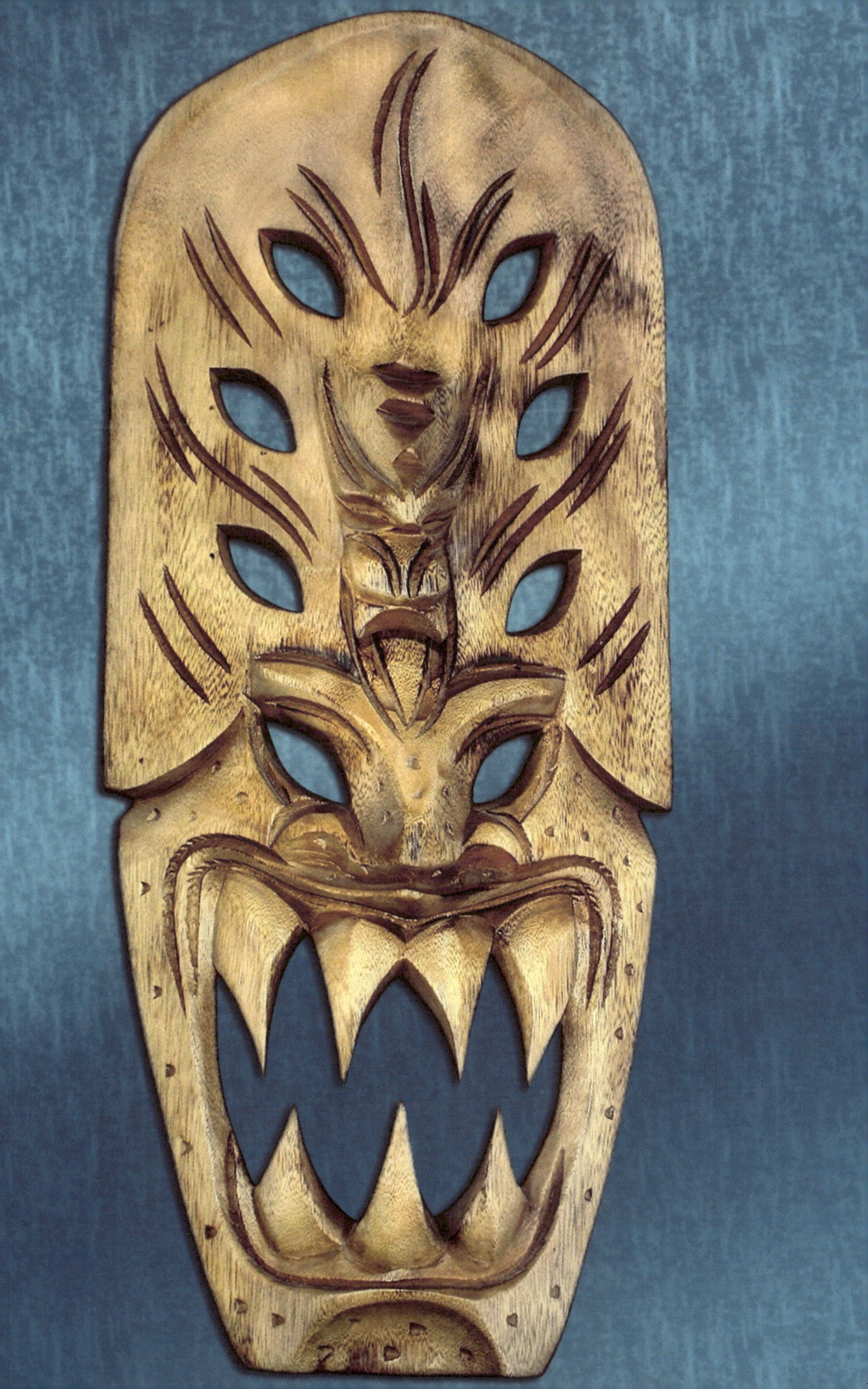

ARTIFACT DESCRIPTION

DESCRIPTION: #17 Philippine Moro Warrior Mask

LENGTH: 8 inches

WIDTH: 3 inches

HEIGHT: 16 inches

COMPOSITION: Wood

COLOR: Dark Brown

COMMENTS: Ferocious

LOCATION OF FIND: Manila Craft Market

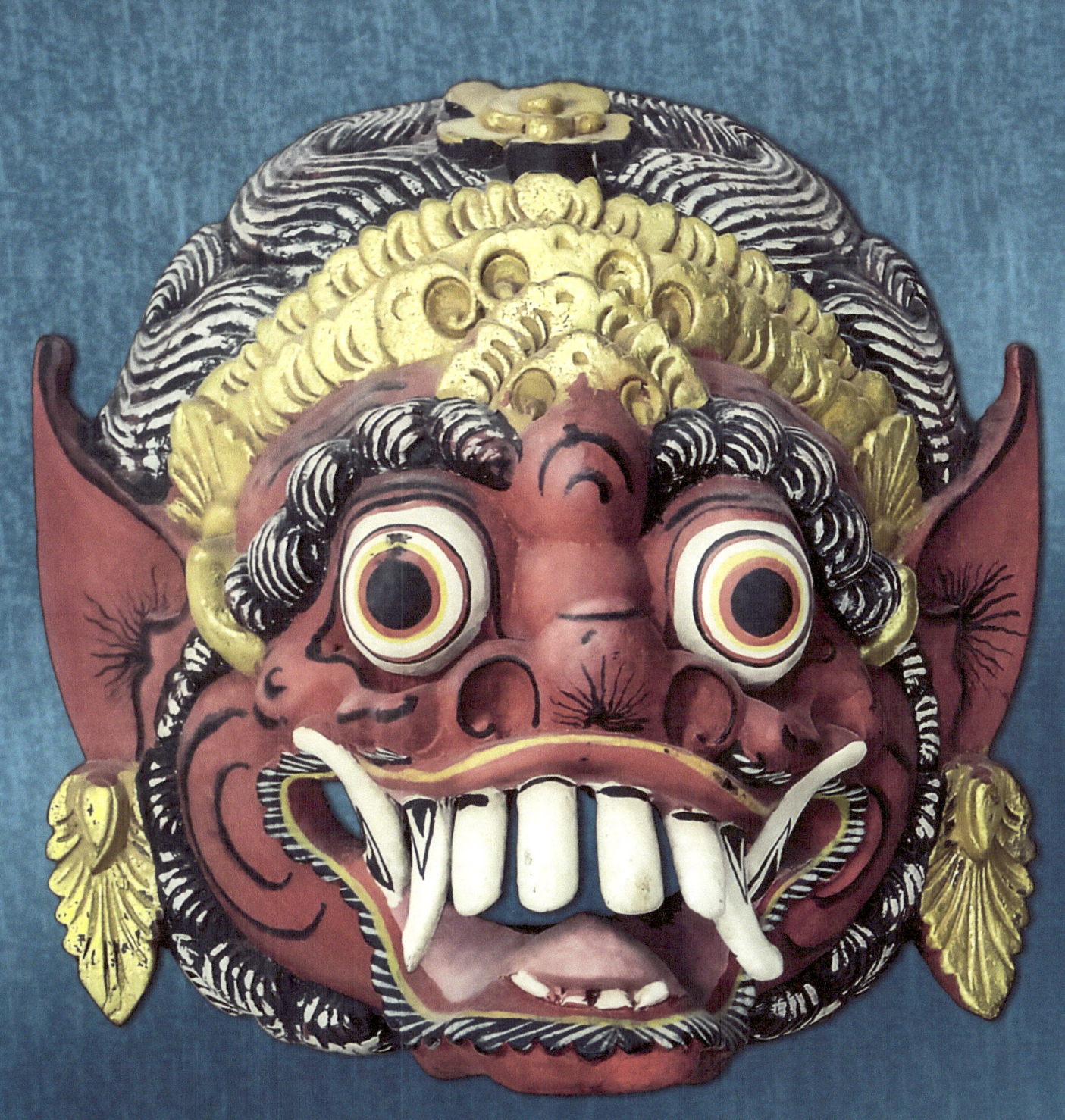

ARTIFACT DESCRIPTION

DESCRIPTION: #18 Indonesian Lion God Theatre Mask

LENGTH: __12 inches__

WIDTH: __2 inches__

HEIGHT: __12 inches__

COMPOSITION: __Wood__

COLOR: __Black, Gold, Red, White and Yellow.__

COMMENTS: __This type of mask is used in theatre plays and for__
__religous ceremonies.__

LOCATION OF FIND: __Flea Market__

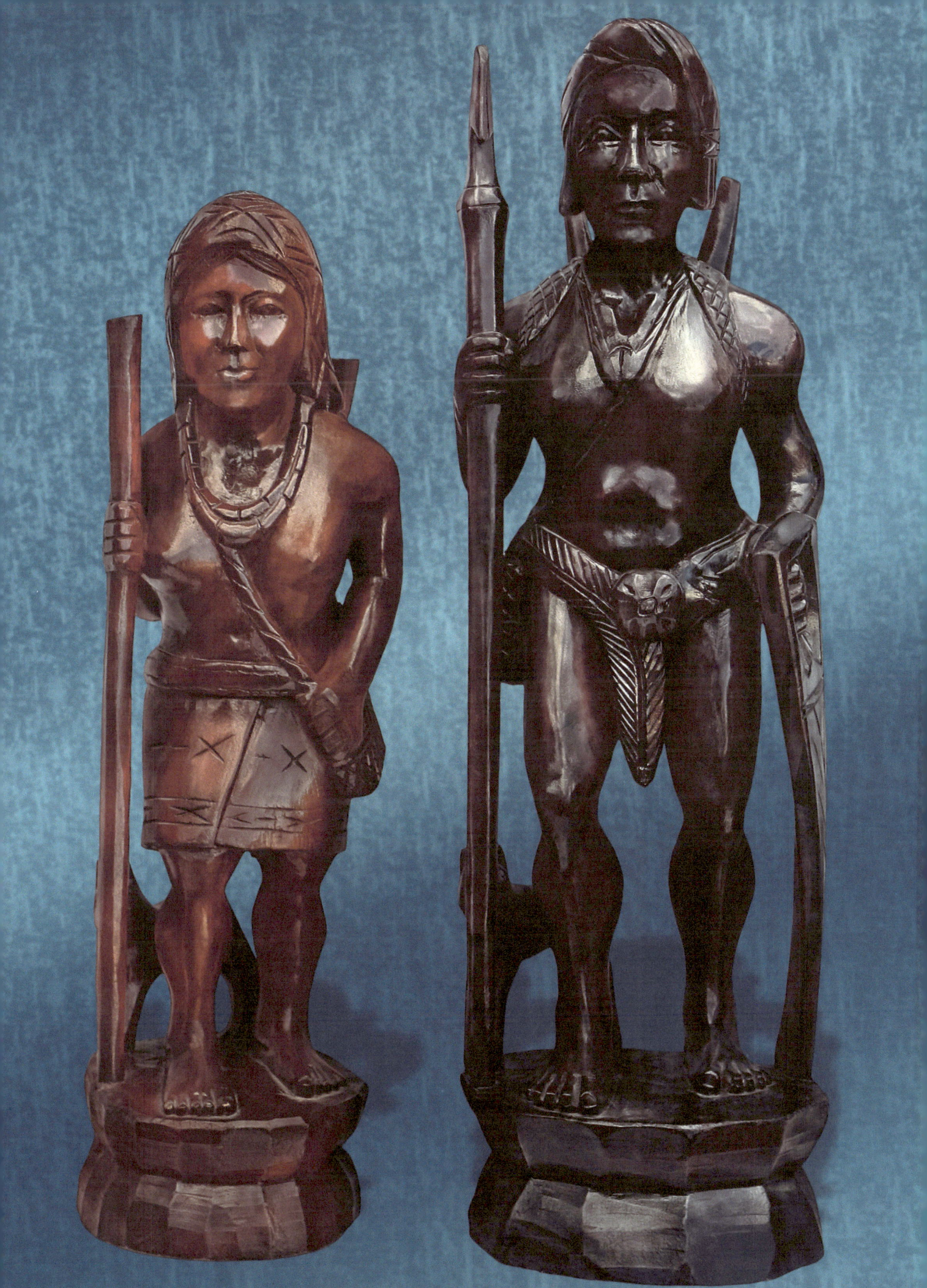

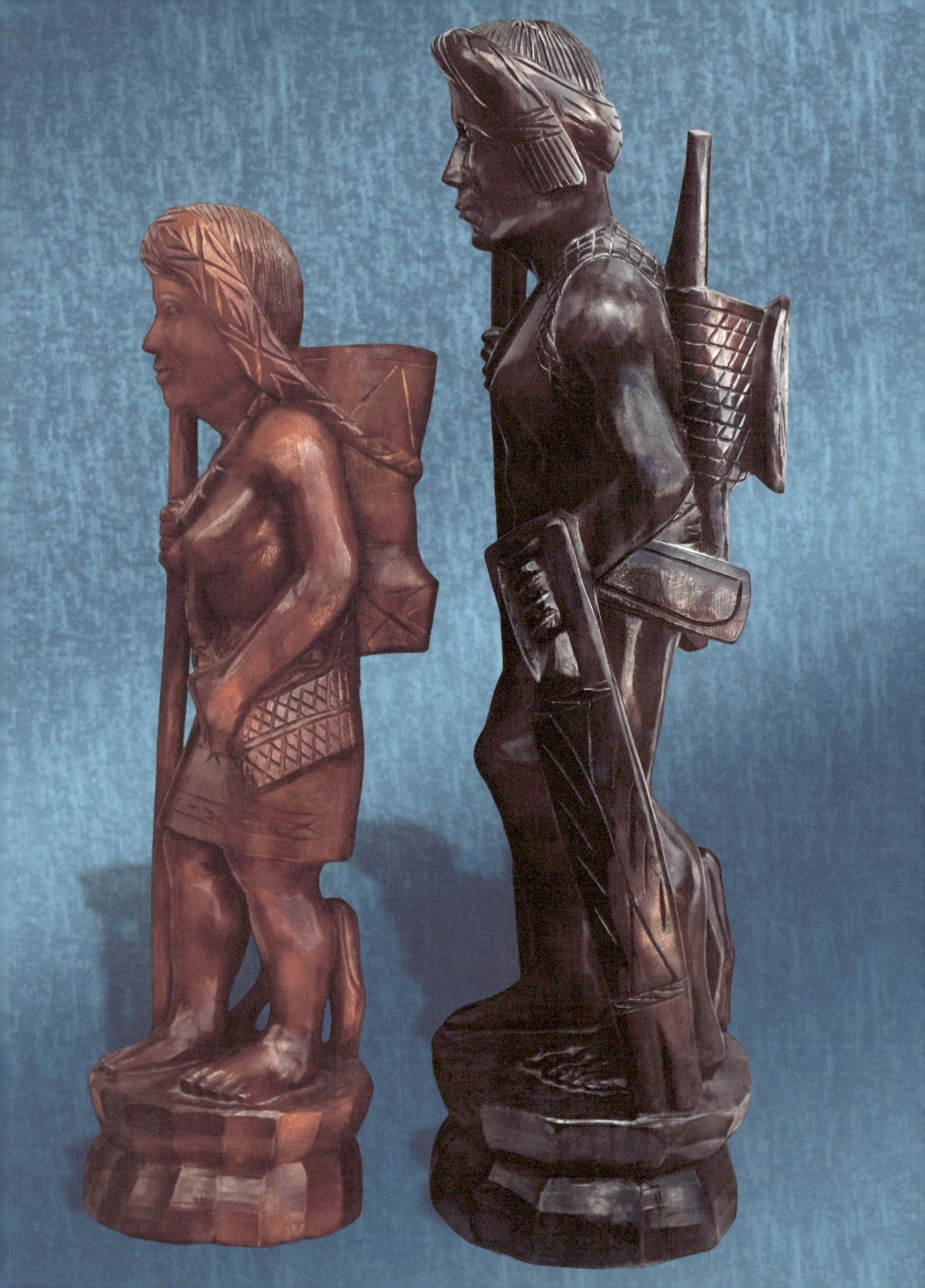

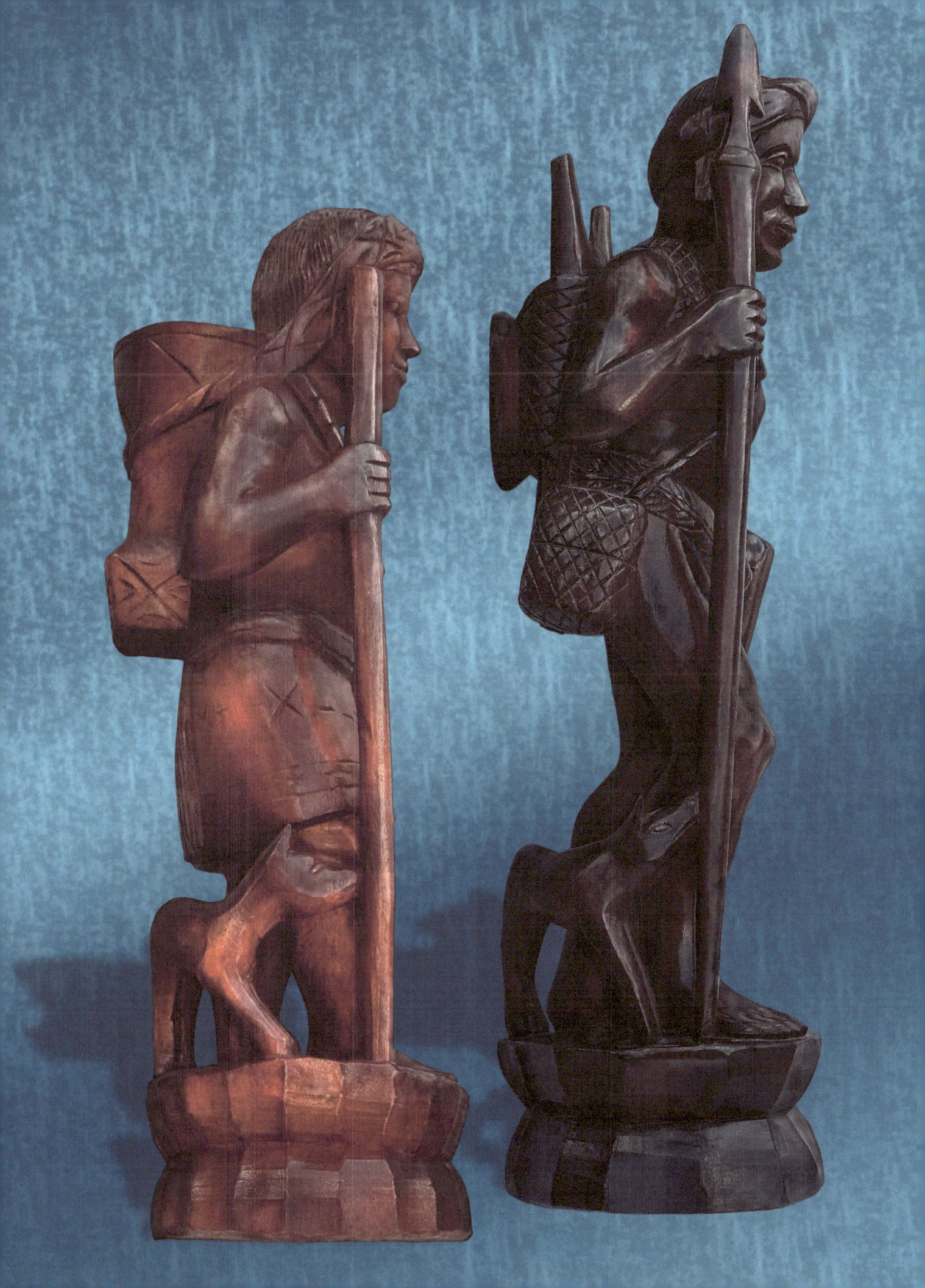

ARTIFACTS of MOROLAND MUSEUM
ARTIFACT DESCRIPTION

DESCRIPTION: #19 Igorot Male and Female Family Warriors

	MALE	FEMALE
LENGTH:	8 inches	6 inches
WIDTH:	8 inches	6 inches
HEIGHT:	26 inches	24 inches
COMPOSITION:	Wood	Wood
COLOR:	Dark Brown	Light Brown

COMMENTS: Male is carrying a hunting pack, shield, spear, and hunting dog.
Female is carrying a food basket, walking stick, and hunting dog.

LOCATION OF FIND: Manila Craft Market

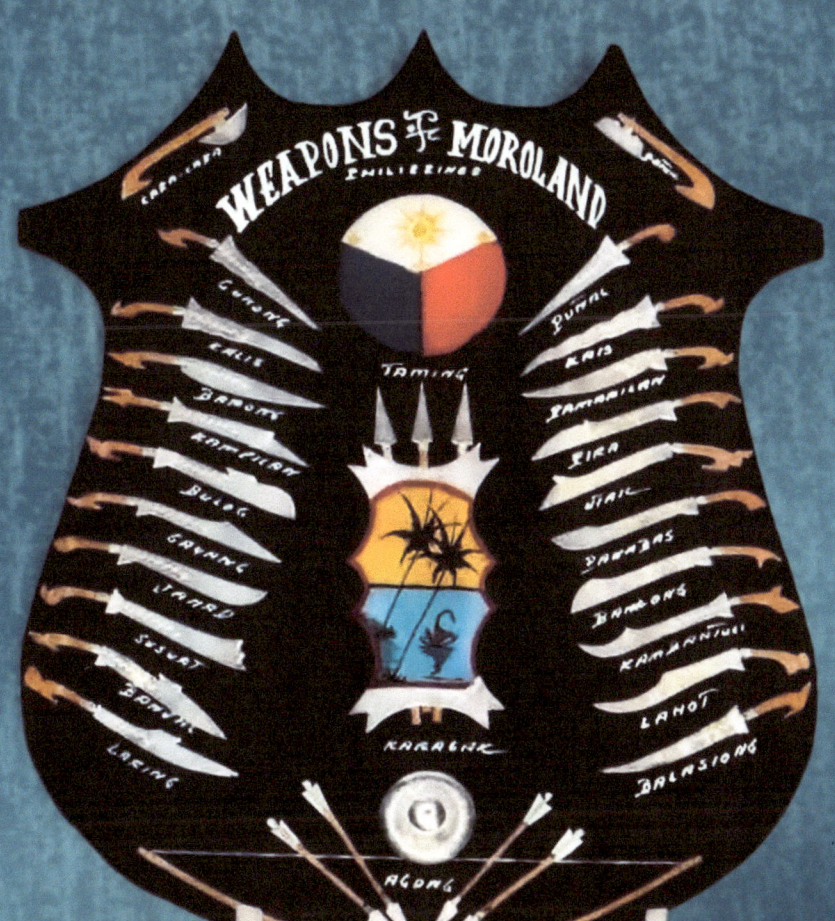

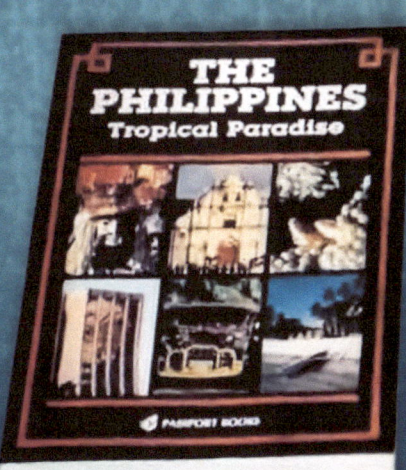

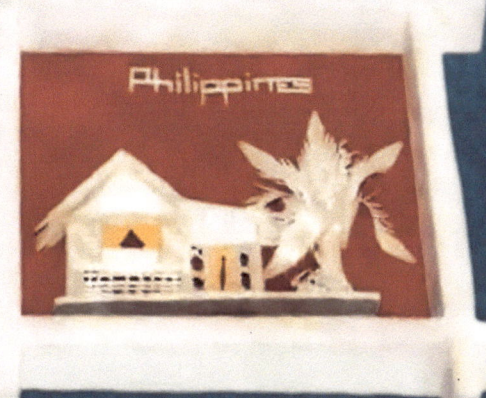

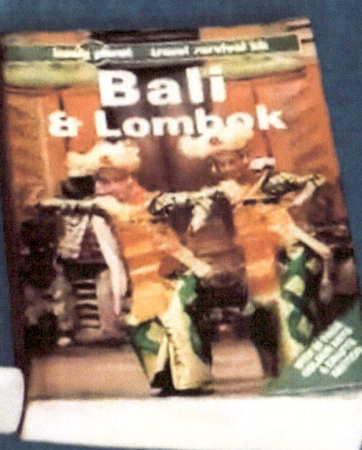

ARTIFACT DESCRIPTION

DESCRIPTION: #20 Philippine Shield with Plaque and Books

LENGTH: 12 inches

WIDTH: 1/4 inch

HEIGHT: 16 inches

COMPOSITION: Wood, Metal, Rope

COLOR: Black, Silver, Red, Blue, Yellow, Green, Brown, Tan, etc

COMMENTS: Excellent help to classify weapons. Very old. W.W.II era.
Plaque and books found in the Philippines.

LOCATION OF FIND: Antique Store

LITTLE EXTRAS

of

MOROLAND MUSEUM

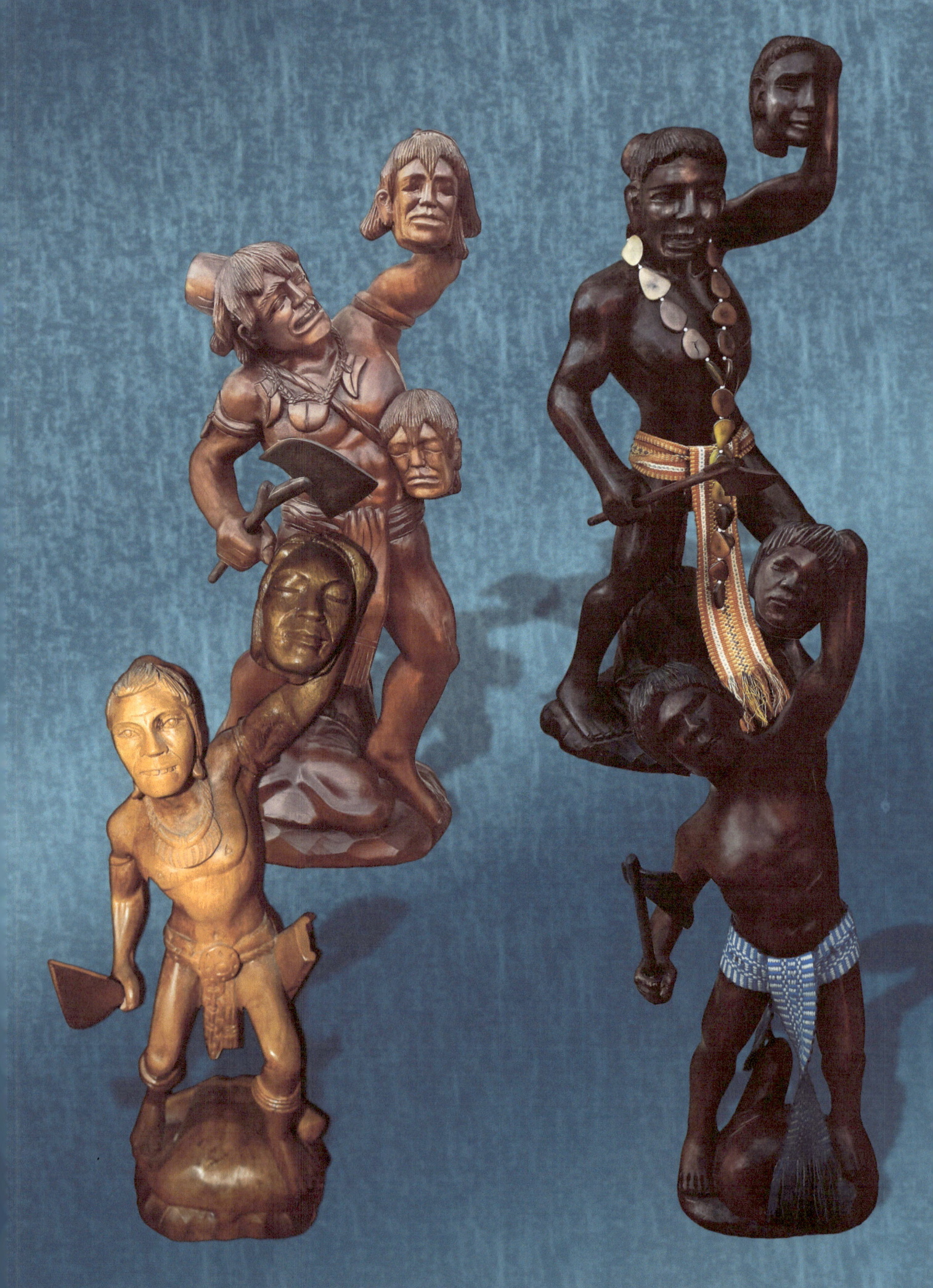

Social

Kumusta?		How are you?	
Ito ang aking...		This is my...	
...anak	...child	...katrabaho	...colleague
...asawa	...husband	...kaibigan	...friend
...asawa	...wife	...kapartner	...partner (intimate)

Nagagalak akong makilala ka. — I'm pleased to meet you.

Sige. — See you later.

Ang pangalan ko ay... — My name is...

Ano ang pangalan mo? — What's your name?

Ano ang tawag nito? — What's this called?

Narito ako para... — I'm here...

...magbakasyon — ...for a holiday
...sa trabaho — ...on business
...mag-aral — ...to study

Dining Out

Ano ang mairerekomenda mo? — What would you recommend?

Pakitawag mo ako ng taksi? — Can you call a taxi for me?

May alam ka bang restoran? — Can you recommend a restaurant?

Gusto ko iyan. — I'll have that.

Gusto kong mag-reserba ng mesa para sa... — I'd like to reserve a table for...

Gaano katagal ang paghihintay? — How long is the wait?

Ano iyan? — What's in that dish?

May bayad ba ang mesa? — Is there a cover charge?

"BAYAN KO"
Golden Philippine Eagle

**IBON MANG MAY LAYANG LUMIPAD
KULUNGIN MO AT UMIIYAK
BAYAN PA KAYANG SAKDAL DILAG
ANG DI MAG NASANG MAKAALPAS**

**PILIPINAS KUNG MINUMUTYA
PUGAD NG LUHA AT DALITA
ATING ADHAKA MAKITA KANG
SAKDAL LAYA.**

THIS TRUE STORY MAY NOT END HAPPILY EVER AFTER...

Once upon a time, thousands of these magnificent creatures flew in skies of the most brilliant shade of blue. Awesome to behold, they reached three feet tall when fully grown. And their wings spanned seven feet long when spread out. Called the Philippine Golden Eagle because they can't be found anywhere else except in our country, these birds made their nests in the trees of rainforest so dense, you could almost lose your way in them. Here clear rivers ran, plants and flowers were plentiful, and other animals roamed freely. These beautiful rainforest were truly the perfect home for these proud, majestic birds. And for many, many years, they lived peacefully and unharmed.

Until something terrible happened. The rainforest -- the only real home of the Philippine Golden Eagles -- were being destroyed by man's greed and wastefulness. As these forests disappeared, so did the eagles, for food and shelter had become scarce to them. Where once thousands of Philippine Golden Eagles flew freely, only about 50 now exists. And yet, they are still in danger. Because the rainforest continue to disappear. One day soon, there will be no more Philippine Eagles.

UNLESS WE DO SOMETHING TO HELP!

Yes we can help the endangered Philippine Golden Eagle. How? By taking good care of our rainforest. That way these creatures are assured of shelter, warm nests and enough food to eat. And because these are the rainforest that give us the clean air we breathe and the water we drink, we'll be helping ourselves as well. Learn more about the Philippine Golden Eagle on the internet or at your local library. And tell your family, friends and teachers about it. After all don't you want the Philippine Golden Eagles to live happily ever after?

SAVE THE GOLDEN PHILIPPINE EAGLE
Author Unknown

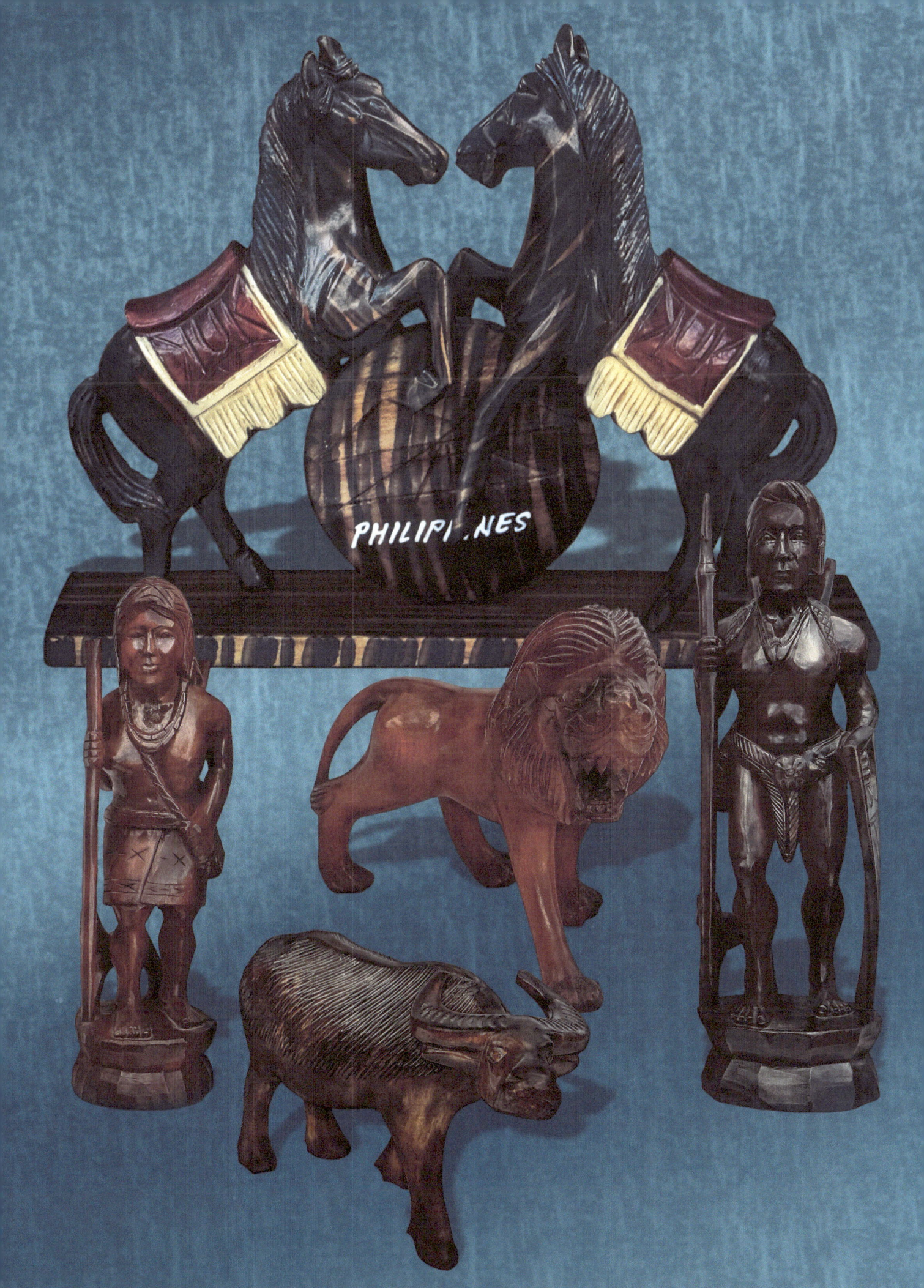

PHILIPI NES

STATEMENTS

The writers of this book intentions were not to claim to be or imply in any way that they are experts or any kind of authority of any country's history, art, language, or weapons.

All items are shown "as is". MOROLAND MUSEUM will not make any representation of warranty, expressed or implied, as to the marketability, fitness or condition of the items shown or described, description, genuineness, attribution, size, provenance, location of origination, or period of the shown items.

The writers would like to say

THANK YOU

to those whose support and input made this book possible.

Our Spouses, Our Children, Our Friends We would also like to thank those curious collectors who before us have preserved this part of our past and those whose skills, patience, and imagination made these items to begin with.

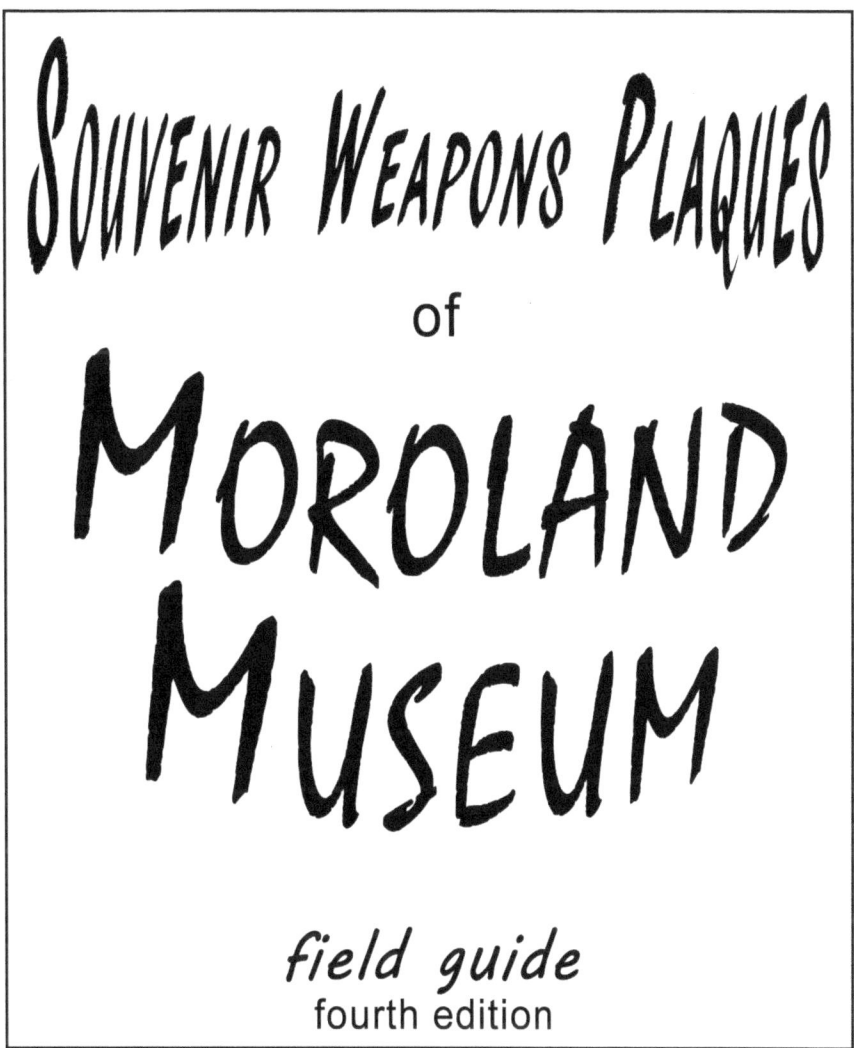

SOUVENIR WEAPONS PLAQUES
of
MOROLAND MUSEUM

field guide
fourth edition

MOROLAND MUSEUM Pictorial Publication's fourth edition has a variety of Moroland Souvenir Weapons Plaques from the Philippines. This pictorial field guide will be a valuable help when on the hunt for an addition to your collection or simply curious. It will have the same style of descriptions that you have come to depend upon. Every items description is conveniently located near to its full color picture like page. It will also have those wonderful extras that you liked so much. This new edition will have a variety of Moroland Souvenir Weapons Plaques for your eyes to admire.

**YOU WILL NEED TO GET THE NEXT EDITION TO
DISCOVER WHAT OTHER DELIGHTS IT HOLDS FOR YOU.**

ARTIFACTS

of

MOROLAND

MUSEUM

field guide
third edition

MOROLAND MUSEUM Pictorial Publication's third edition has a variety of Phillipine artifacts for your eyes to admire. This pictorial field guide is a valuable help when on the hunt for an addition to your collection or simply curious. It has the same style of descriptions that you have come to depend upon. Every items description is conveniently located near to its full color picture. It has those wonderful extras that you liked so much.

YOU WILL NEED TO GET THE NEXT EDITION TO
DISCOVER WHAT OTHER DELIGHTS IT HOLDS FOR YOU.